THE HOW TO

Start And Maintain A Church Prayer Ministry Or Prayer Group

PRAYER MANUAL

DR. MELROSE BETHEA

THE HOW TO PRAYER MANUAL

Copyright 2025 by Melrose Bethea
All Rights Reserved.

ISBN: 978-1-950315-11-6

This book or parts thereof may not be reproduced in any form, stored in a retrieval system, or transmitted in any form by any means electronic, mechanical, photocopy, recording, or otherwise for commercial gain or profit without prior written permission of the publisher. The use of short quotations or occasional page copying for personal or group study is permitted and encouraged.

Published by:
GOD'S LIFE PUBLISHING
Phone Number: 973 986-5407
5369 Edgewater Dr. Ewa Beach, HI 96706
Web: www.godslifepublishing.org
Email: godlife@aol.com

Designed by:
God's Life Publishing

Cover Design:
Calvin L. Bethea

Unless otherwise identified, Scripture quotations are from the Authorized King James Version of the Bible.

Printed in the United States of America

DEDICATION

This prayer manual is dedicated to the Holy Spirit so that he may use it to advance the work of the kingdom. Without his aid and help over these many years prior to this writing, what is on these pages would not have existed.

I would also like to dedicate this work to the many prayer warriors and intercessors around our nation who tirelessly remain on the walls to make up the hedge in prayer. May this volume recruit many more warriors to the holy ministry of intercession.

God's Life Christian Church congregation, thank you for collaborating with the Holy Spirit to fulfill his 2007 vision of establishing a local church prayer ministry. Praying the scriptures was a new and challenging concept for many. With perseverance, you all stayed the course, breaking many strongholds, freeing captives, changing the community, and aligning governmental agencies toward a more godlier approach in their work.

My sincere appreciation goes to my husband and ministry partner, Bishop Calvin Bethea, for his encouragement and prayers. You showed me the value of providing this tool to those who need help with their prayer ministry. Your unwavering faith and confidence bolstered my faith to complete this prayer manual. Thank you!

TABLE OF CONTENTS

Preface	7
Introduction	11
The Need For Corporate Prayer	13
-Scriptural Basis	15
-The Benefits	17
-How to Organize Corporate Prayer	21
Month One: Return To Prayer	23
Month Two: Seek To Go A Little Farther In Your Prayer Relationship	31
Month Three: Humble Yourself	37
Month Four: Internalize God's Word	43
Month Five: Grow In Grace	49
Month Six: Be Biblically Transformed	57
Month Seven: Submit To God	65
Month Eight: Trust God, He Is Faithful	71
Month Nine: Serve God Acceptably	77
Month Ten: Be Ye Holy, For I Am Holy	83
Month Eleven: Live A Biblical Worldview	89
Month Twelve: Let's Take This City	95
Final Words	101
About The Author	103

PREFACE

HOW TO USE THIS MANUAL

The Holy Spirit directed the co-author to write this manual to guide and establish a vibrant prayer ministry in your church or prayer group that transforms lives, deepens your relationship with God and one another. This comprehensive resource equips you with practical tools, invaluable insights, and uplifting spiritual principles essential for cultivating a thriving intercessory prayer group. You will discover the essential steps to spark a renewed passion for prayer within your congregation or group. It will further build your confidence in the word of God as you see unity and success in your prayer efforts. As you develop the habit of searching the scriptures for pertinent promises for your situation, praying those scriptures and looking to Jesus, the author and finisher of your faith, you will fulfill God's plan for your life and advance the kingdom of God.

PREPARATIONS FOR THE PRAYER LEADER:

The church or group leader should select a designated prayer start and finish times. You can alter the time based on the Holy Spirit's leading. Begin by setting aside at least one hour to pray.

A prayer leader can be assigned for the group or be selected each time you gather to assist everyone in staying on task while they pray. Everyone taking part does not have to pray, but he or she should be prepared to pray.

The prayer leader should always reference the first month's sample prayer focus as a guide of what the leader should do to guide the intercessors weekly.

RESPONSIBILITIES FOR THE PRAYER LEADERS:

Provide a copy of the prayer focus for that month to each participant. It would also be beneficial for each person to have their own personal manual.

Prepare in advance two to three target areas you would like the group to pray using the weekly prayer topic for that month

Read the theme for the month, introduction for the prayer, and the subject for that week of prayer.

Briefly define any terms that may be unfamiliar in the introduction.

Read the scripture to be prayed, and invite everyone to join in a circle to pray in unity.

Prayer leader will have a brief opening prayer of thankfulness for the opportunity to pray and for a successful prayer meeting.

Following the opening prayer, the leader will call on an individual as the Spirit leads them to pray the scriptures concerning a specific area where the group is requesting divine intervention. After one person prays, another person can be called to target a different aspect of the prayer focus.

If for any reason the prayer is drifting off course, the leader may interrupt and redirect everyone back on course. Only the person who is called on is to pray. Everyone else in the circle should agree with the prayers with limited vocal interaction while they are listening.

The prayer leader closes out the prayer with thanksgiving (see Philippians 4:6) by faith that God will reward and give answers to meet the prayer request (see Hebrews 11:6).

Preparation For Individuals Participating In Corporate Prayer:

This is a list of things each participant should do before he or she gathers with the prayer group to assure good success in his or her prayer efforts.

1. Study the prayer focus before you gather with your prayer group
2. Meditate on the topic and scripture.
3. Come early to help you make the switch from your busy day to spiritual things.
4. Enter into the church or gathering place with thanksgiving
5. Have an expectation for God to pour out his Spirit.
6. Agree with the scriptures and the person praying.
7. Believe God's word, be specific and direct in what you pray.

Each month of this manual is carefully designed with a weekly prayer focus, featuring:

Monthly Theme:

A theme is chosen for each month to anchor your prayers and intentions as you fulfill Jesus' command to pray always. These topics were chosen by the Holy Spirit to lead us back to a lifestyle of prayer and a burden for the needs of others.

Introduction To Prayer Topic:

A brief overview of the subject is provided to ensure each participant can come into agreement as they take part in the prayer.

Specific Prayer Focus For Each Week:

Each week has a focus that is taken from the introduction. The target areas each month will focus on prayer for Christians, church leaders, governmental leaders, sinners and families. These areas are broad enough for you to include the specific needs of your local church and community.

A Sample Prayer For Each Month:

A sample prayer is included for each month to demonstrate how and what to petition God for.

Instructions For The Prayer Leader:

Each month there will be instructions in the sample prayer for the prayer leader.

Prayers Based on Specific Scripture:

You are provided with a list of the specific scriptures referenced in the sample prayer. Since God watches over his word to perform it, these scriptures teach you God's word and enable you to give God back his word in prayer. It will also increase your faith and confidence in God's Word as you pray. Reading these scriptures in advance will prepare your heart and mind for your intercessory group prayer. You may also use these scriptures to pray in your private time at home before you meet with the group.

INTRODUCTION

This book serves as a prayer tool for the local church or any group wanting to pray more effectively. There is a prayer crisis in the church today. Though the church is full of activities, streams of people going in and out and all kinds of programs, there is often no scheduled time for corporate prayer. Jesus declared in Matthew 21:13, *"My house (church) shall be called the house of prayer; but you have made it a den of thieves."* Unfortunately, in those days and even today, God's house is more like a den of thieves than it is a house of prayer. Many people gathering together in the church have ulterior motives. They don't just gather for spiritual purposes. Some are showing up to hand out their business cards; others are there with their sales pitch to prey on the leaders or members; and there are some who are there to spy out the liberties given to believers in Christ. Without intercessory prayer, the dependency on Christ, the unity of the congregation, and the advancement of the kingdom suffer, are delayed, and even cease to exist. Therefore, the Church must restore intercessory prayer to its rightful place to regain its former glory. We must remove the brass and copper (the unholy mixture) and usher in the gold (holy things).

It is my earnest belief that God desires his house (church) to return to making prayer a priority. When I speak of prayer being a priority, I mean that it should precede everything else; it must be held in a higher regard than other things, and it must be viewed as more important than any other thing. Prayer must be at the top of our list of things that we ought to pursue and make a part of our daily Christian walk. In the beginning of chapter six of Matthew, Jesus answered his disciple's question of how they should pray by sharing with them the Lord's Prayer. He further told them in verse thirty-six to, *"seek first the kingdom of God, and all his righteousness; and all these things shall be added unto you."* Jesus completed his instruction to the disciples by letting them know that prayer must be their priority. He further implies that the very thing that they should seek first, not second or third, must be prayer. Prayer should not be used just when there is an emergency, a quick blessing for a meal to impress onlookers, or as part of a ritual, protocol or program that is hurried and with no reverence to the one that is being addressed. The most valuable tool that our heavenly Father has given to us for daily use in the morning (see Psalm 5:3), in the evening (see Psalm 55:17) and at midnight (see Psalm 119:62) is prayer. Through prayer, we have direct communication and fellowship with our heavenly Father. It is to be relied upon in every challenge we may find ourselves in. The most blessed result of talking to and listening to our heavenly Father is the transformation that takes place in us. Our prayers change us. This indeed is good news. The ultimate goal of prayer is to change you and me; not to change God. Prayer enables us to be transformed in our minds to the perfect will of Almighty God so that we can be workers together with him in making Jesus known to a lost and dying world.

Jesus has left the church as his instrument of intercession in the world. Even as Jesus is the great mediator between God and man (1 Timothy 2:5), the church acts as a visible entity on the earth to stand in the gap between God and sinful men through prayer. The early church began by having a prayer meeting that ushered in a revival of repentance that brought thousands to God's saving grace. In the Book of Acts, one hundred and twenty average men and women who were fearful, doubtful and without hope for the future gathered in the upper room in obedience to Jesus' last instruction to wait for the promise. They were unknown to the world and without titles or position. They gathered in one accord in prayer and supplication, **got a hold of God** as they prayed and were never the same. Immediate miraculous changes took place in their lives. An impetuous, unlearned, anxious, hot-headed fisherman named Peter was transformed by prayer into a bold but humble, eloquent speaker exhibiting patience and fortitude in declaring and proclaiming the truth of God's word. This group of believers became knitted together in a unified body that would in a short time turn the known world upside down for Christ in their lifestyle and witness.

Our current world has need of a church and prayer groups of men and women that would get a hold of God in prayer and supplication that would turn our nation and the uttermost parts of the world upside down for Christ. The early church's continual prayer brought an increase in souls being saved, broke down racial barriers, and showed the power of God to religious organizations. The Holy Spirit empowered ordinary men to evangelize boldly, accompanied by signs and wonders. The very foundation of any Bible-believing church must be prayer. As it was in the early church, so must it also be today. Prayer is the change that is needed in our nation in this hour. Change will not come through the White House; it is going to come through a church house or a group of believers that will pray. If a revival is going to come, the church must return to the example of the early church and pray together for one another and in one accord.

THE NEED FOR INTERCESSORY PRAYER IN THE CHURCH

Let us begin by identifying what intercessory prayer is. Intercessory prayer is when multiple people, formally or casually, unite in prayer for a shared need, acknowledging the value of collective faith. Christians may also use intercessory prayer when they have a specific request and feel too weak to exercise faith to receive an answer from God. When a group gathers to share a burden, God often pours out special blessings on them that individuals praying alone don't receive. In Matthew 18:20, Jesus taught the disciples: *"For where two or three are gathered together in my name, there am I in the midst of them"*. Jesus said he would be in the midst. Therefore, his presence will cause an outpouring of additional blessings and anointing upon the group as they pray. He invites and expects every believer to intercede. Intercessory prayer is for all Christians.

For example:

In the game of poker, four of a kind beats a full house every time. The same principle holds true for prayer. More power exists in the prayers of four believers who petition God in unity than in a house full of believers who pray with clashing agendas and attitudes.

The apostles knew that unified prayer with others would keep the governing leaders from fulfilling their threats to block God's work from continuing. They prayed in the upper room and from house to house. Many of us at various times may feel threatened by our boss, manager, gangs, or some person. It is in times like this that we need the power of God to be seen. Intercessory prayer is the agent that brings the power or presence of God into our midst to calm the storms within us as well as to touch others. The apostles took a stand because of intercessory prayer. It is as if they said, "God, at any cost, we are going on with you! All we need is your help!" These disciples weren't praying for comfort; they were praying to meet God's approval. They desired to do the will of God, but recognized they needed boldness and confidence to come forth and do the acceptable will of God. In Acts 1:9, Jesus commanded the apostles and disciples to be witnesses. They were now praying to be faithful and to do what they had been told to do. The church today must follow this example to pray corporately so that we too would do what we were told. Through intercessory prayer, the world, false religion and cults will see Jesus, and the church will be triumphant!

Intercessory prayer brings the manifested power of God in the midst of the gathering. In Acts 4:14-35, authorities arrested and threatened Peter and John for preaching and teaching God's word. Upon their reunion with their fellow Christians, they prayed, lifting their voices to God with one accord. *"And when they had prayed, the place was shaken where they were assembled together (v 31)."* God, came in the midst and provided them with visible proof he was there to answer, strengthen and fill their mouth to speak his word. If we want God to shake the world or others, we must invite him to shake us first! We must allow Christ to work in us, ruffle our feathers, and bring us to humility and total dependence on him. God will not do a work through you until he has done a work in you.

Acts 16:25-34 provides another example of God's manifested power through intercessory prayer. While imprisoned the apostle Paul and Silas prayed and sang praises unto God. There was a great earthquake, so that the foundations of the prison were shaken. Not only did the doors of the prison swing open, but the doors of the heart of the keeper of the prison and his family were now open to salvation. In Second Chronicles 16:9, the author makes it clear that God wants to come into your situation and bring an awesome move of deliverance. He states, *"For the eyes of the Lord run to and fro throughout the whole earth, to show Himself strong in the behalf of them whose heart is perfect toward Him."* God is looking for the opportunity to show himself strong in someone's life and or in the life of his church. His manifested presence will be visible to the sinner and the Christian. God will show up and show off in such a way there will be no denial that we have caught his eye by our praying. If you are born again and part of a local church, you have a duty to gather together and pray with others for others.

SCRIPTURAL BASIS FOR INTERCESSORY PRAYER:

Many times in scripture, the various writers used a variety of phrases to speak about prayer. Phrases like, "cried unto the Lord, call upon the Lord, ask help of the Lord, lift up their voice," are all references to prayer. There are several examples in the Old Testament and the New Testament of corporate prayer that brought great mercy and deliverance to Israel and the early church. Since Jesus is the same yesterday, today and tomorrow (see Hebrews 13:8), he will always honor and respond to the unified prayer of his people. It is the Father's good pleasure to give us the answers to our petitions. Let us look at the examples below.

Numbers 20:16 *"And when we cried unto the Lord, he heard our voice, and sent an angel, and hath brought us forth out of Egypt: and, behold, we are in Kadesh, a city in the uttermost of thy borders"*

2 Chronicles 20:4-30 *"And Judah gathered themselves together, to ask help of the Lord: the Lord fought against the enemies of Israel".*

Joel 1:14, 2:17-18 *"Sanctify ye a fast, call a solemn assembly, gather the elders and all the inhabitants of the land into the house of the Lord your God, and cry unto the Lord. Let the priests, the ministers of the LORD, weep between the porch and the altar, and let them say, Spare thy people O LORD, and give not thine heritage to reproach, that the heathen should rule over them: wherefore should they say among the people, Where **is** their God? Then will the LORD be jealous for his land, and pity his people. Yea, the LORD will answer and say unto his people, Behold, I will send you corn, and wine, and oil, and ye shall be satisfied therewith: and I will no more make you a reproach among the heathen:"*

Jonah 3:8-10 *But let man and beast be covered with sackcloth, and cry mightily unto God: ...And God saw their works, that they turned from their evil way; and God repented of the evil, that he had said that he would do unto them; and he did it not.*

Acts 1:14, 2:2-4 *These all continued with one accord in prayer and supplication, And suddenly there came a sound from heaven as of a rushing mighty wind, and it filled all the house where they were sitting. And they were all filled with the Holy Ghost, and began to speak with other tongues, as the Spirit gave them utterance.*

Acts 4:24-31 *And when they heard that, they lifted up their voice to God with one accord grant unto thy servants, that with all boldness they may speak thy word. And when they had prayed the place was shaken where they were assembled together and they were all filled with the Holy Ghost, and they spake the word of God with boldness.*

Acts 12:5-17 *Peter therefore was kept in prison: but prayer was made without ceasing of the church unto God for him. But he, declared unto them how the Lord had brought him out of the prison.*

Matthew 18:20 *For where two or three are gathered together in my name, there am I in the midst of them.*

Since God is in the addition and multiplication business, it would seem to me that if I get one other person to agree with me in prayer, we will definitely see the manifestation of the answers quicker. These verses above show that God doesn't need a multitude of individuals to pray; just two or more will be sufficient.

THE BENEFITS OF INTERCESSORY PRAYER

One benefit of intercessory prayer is its ability to unite believers. There is a story about the redwood tree that can help us understand the unity that this kind of prayer will solidify. A redwood tree, when it grows to maturity, reaches a height of one hundred feet. Yet, a redwood's roots usually only reach depths between six and twelve inches. So why doesn't a mild wind topple a redwood? It's because the roots of individual redwood trees embrace and intertwine. They grab on to one another and never let go. That's how redwoods stand; they stand together like a team. God likewise designed the church to be a unified force on earth, standing together so that no weapon formed against individual members or the whole body can prosper.

The unity of the church should be a driving passion because everyone who is born again has the same Spirit, serves the same Lord and has the same hope. In his letter to the church at Ephesus, the apostle Paul encouraged the believers there with these words, *"There is one body, and one Spirit, even as ye are called one hope of your calling; One Lord, one faith, one baptism, One God and Father of all, who is above all, and through all, and in you all"* (Ephesians 4:1-6). Corporate prayer's ultimate purpose is "so that the body of Christ may be built up in the faith and knowledge of the Son of God and become mature, attaining to the whole measure of the fullness of Christ" (Ephesians 4:11-16).

Intercessory prayer will get rid of the isms and schisms in the Body of Christ. If there is any jealousy or strife, that too will disappear. In Acts 4:24, the disciples lifted their voices to God with one accord, so God would be glorified in their witness. Because of their prayer, their hearts was knitted in unity, *"And the multitude of them that believed were of one heart and of one soul: neither said any of them that ought of the things which he possessed was his own; but they had all things common. and great grace was upon them all. Neither was there any among that lacked: for as many as were possessors of lands or houses sold them, and brought the prices of the things that were sold,... And distribution was made unto every man according as he had need"* (Acts 4:32-35). God not only got into their hearts, he got into their pocketbooks and their checkbooks. God was able to put himself on display to an unbelieving world all because the early church practiced intercessory prayer. Likewise, the world needs to see Jesus in this hour pouring his great grace upon his church.

Another benefit of intercessory prayer is that it produces a dependency on the body of Christ. Many times, we want to live with a Lone Ranger mentality in our prayer life. We think all our prayers must be secretive and only for God's ear. According to the scriptures, Jesus told us that sometimes we must get into our secret closet to pray (see Matthew 6: 6), but in Matthew 18:20, he is telling us that there are also times that we need other people to pray with us. The apostle Paul had confidence that intercessory prayer would strengthen and enable him to preach the gospel more effectively. He counted on the prayers of the local church and was willing to write to them of his need for prayer. He was not embarrassed to admit his need for intercessory prayer. Neither was he a fool to think that he was an island unto himself. The apostle Paul knew God surrounded him with others who would gird him up in prayer. His trust was in God's ability to hear and send the answers that would cause the work assigned to him to prosper (see Matthew 18:19). Let us look at some of the apostle Paul's requests for intercessory prayer from the saints in the various churches he had planted.

> **Romans 15:30-32** *-strive with me in your prayers to God for me that I may be delivered and my service be acceptable to the saints in Jerusalem.*
>
> **2 Corinthians 1:8-11** *Ye also helping together by prayer for us, (to be delivered out of trouble in Asia)*
>
> **Ephesians 6:18-19** *Praying always..And for me, that utterance may be given unto me, that I may open my mouth boldly, to make known the mystery of the gospel.*
>
> **Philippians 1:19** *For I know that this shall turn to my salvation through your prayer,*
>
> **Colossians 4:3** *Praying also for us, that God would open unto us a door of utterance to speak the mystery of Christ,*
>
> **2 Thessalonians 3:1-2** *Finally brethren, pray for us, that the word of the Lord may have free course, and be glorified, even as it is with you: And that we may be delivered from unreasonable and wicked men: for all men have not faith.*
>
> **1 John 5:14-15** *And this is the confidence that we have in him, that, if we ask anything according to his will, he heareth us; And if we know that he hear us, whatsoever we ask, we know that we have the petitions that we desired of him.*

Intercessory prayer also produces quick answers to our prayer requests. Over the years, I have witnessed quick answers to prayer when we used intercessory prayer for personal needs and church matters. I first noticed this twenty years ago. The Lord led my husband and me to plant a church in our home in 1992. So, we converted our basement into a sanctuary. Our fellowship was just a few faithful families who loved the Lord and wanted to honor him. Our pastor (Calvin Bethea) became burdened with counselling families affected by the effects of alcohol abuse. To complicate matters, there was a bar in our community. As a matter of fact, it was around the corner from our house on a major street. The alcohol abuse resulted in street fights, created financial troubles in marriages and abandonment of children. Pastor Bethea began to pray and ask the Lord for a strategic plan that would address this problem. God gave him instructions to search out the scriptures that addressed all of his concerns with this situation. It took him and me a few days to get the scriptures written out. Then the Lord told him to invite five members to come to the sanctuary to pray. Once everyone was assembled, God told him to share the negative effects of the bar in our community. He also shared his desire for the bar to close. He had printed out copies of the scriptures for everyone. We read them together, and our pastor instructed us to gather in a circle, hold hands, and take turns praying the scriptures we had searched out. Within a month, the entire strip mall that housed the bar was closed. God then instructed our pastor to move the church to the part of the building that was used for the bar. This was not a simple task for us in our minds. We only had a few members, some were battling drug addiction and had no jobs others were retired and living on social security, we had no savings towards a rent and no credit to get a bank loan for renovations and refurbishing this bar into God's house. Again, we searched the scriptures and prayed together. We applied and received the variance that was needed from city officials in record time. Through intercessory prayer, God provided the resources, labor and finances that were needed to transform a dirty, dingy bar into a majestic house for God. Our pastor did most of the work in the evenings when he came from work. These things took about six months to be accomplished. Again, this church had no building fund, no financier, and did not solicit any special offering. This was a miracle that occurred only because of intercessory prayer.

Leviticus 26:8 illustrates the principle that two are better than one: *"five can chase one hundred and one hundred can put ten thousand to flight"*. I remember a time when one brother in the church needed a job. He had been searching for months with no success. All the doors seemed closed. On a Friday night when the men met for fellowship, he brought it to their attention and asked for everyone present to pray with him for a job that would work around the church services and would enable him to meet his financial responsibilities. The following week he reported he had gotten a good job that would not interfere with his commitment to serve in the church. Because two or three were gathered in unity, it invited God to work in the situation. The collective prayer of a unified group proved more effective and faster than individual prayer.

HOW SHOULD YOU ORGANIZE FOR INTERCESSORY PRAYER?

I suggest your prayer group use one chapter from this manual each month on the subject in need of prayer. Use each weekly prayer meeting to concentrate on one focus for the month when you meet. It is beneficial for there to be a designated prayer leader selected for each time your group meets. It will be their responsibility to bring everyone into one accord, reiterating the gathering's purpose, reviewing the prayer focus, reading the introduction and scripture references, and leading everyone to approach the throne of grace. Only one person should be called upon to pray at any time; everyone else should agree with the person praying. The prayer leader will then call on someone else as the Spirit would direct them to pray. Everyone does not have to be given an opportunity to pray. The emphasis is that everyone believes God, that their prayers will agree with God's will for the subject, change them and change others. God has sought and is still seeking a person to make up the hedge. What you are gathering to do is to make yourselves available as a conduit through which the Holy Spirit can pray the Father's will through. This is indeed a wonderful privilege.

The format I will suggest is to use the same theme for an entire month. The areas to focus on during intercessory prayer will concentrate on prayer for the Body of Christ, Christian leaders, governmental leaders, family and sinners. Begin by meditating on the scriptures before you gather to pray. Allow the Lord to add additional scriptures to the ones given. Please note this is not a worship meeting, so limit singing to one hymn or praise song or nothing at all. This is also not a preaching opportunity for the one leading prayer, so refrain from preaching and use the designated time to pray. Many people talk about prayer, sing about prayer and yet never pray. Prayer is only prayer if we pray!

Preparations before you meet:

1. Study the prayer focus before you gather with your prayer group
2. Arrive early to help adjust your mind and heart for the mission
3. Enter into the church or your meeting place with thanksgiving
4. Have an expectation for God to move
5. Agree with the scriptures and the person praying
6. Believe God's word, be specific and direct in what you pray
7. Ponder the following verses as you prepare:

James 5:16b *The effectual fervent prayer of a righteous man availeth much.*

Hebrews 11:6 *But without faith it is impossible to please him, for he that cometh to God must believe that he is, and that he is a rewarder of them that diligently seek him.*

Matthew 18:19 *Again I say unto you, That if two of you shall agree on earth as touching anything that they shall, it shall be done for them of my Father which is in heaven.*

MONTH 1

RETURN TO PRAYER

"Let us search and try our ways, and turn again to the Lord" (Lamentations 3:40).

"Continue in prayer, and watch in the same with thanksgiving" (Colossians 4:2).

No person is greater than his or her prayer life; and no church is greater than its prayer life. The current state of the church concerning prayer is dismal. Many churches do not have a scheduled prayer meeting as part of the weekly service schedule. Prayer is often thrown in as part of the worship service, or part of the Sunday school teaching, and part of the opening protocol before church outings. Now more than ever, the trumpet is sounding in Zion. The Lord is calling all those in his army to man the battlefields with intercessory prayer. Our opponent is a man of war from his departure out of heaven. He is fierce, tenacious, deceptive, calculating, and evil to the core. The same liar that was in the Garden of Eden is still ensnaring us with the question, Did God say? Jesus has given us the offensive strategy. Though our enemy is trying to sneak through our backdoor with his lies, we are to go into his front door and subdue his evil works with prayer. The scriptures command us to pray without ceasing, to pray with fervency, and to pray always with all prayer and supplication in the Spirit (see Ephesians 6:18, 1 Thessalonians 5:17). Thus, we must be in constant communion or communication with the Father, if we are to expect a revival in our prayer life. We have the word of prayer and the ministry of prayer; let us use this amazing privilege and pray.

The great theologian and prayer warrior Leonard Ravenhill in his book, *Why Revival Tarries* stated the condition of the church as follows, *"There are many organizers and few agonizers, many players and payers and few pray-ers, many choirs and few travailers, lots of preachers and few wrestlers, many fears and few tears, much fashion and little passion, many interferers and few intercessors, many entertainers and few believers, many sleepers and few watchers."*

Week 1

Pray For Christians To Return To A Lifestyle of Prayer

Read: Exodus 32:9-14

Meditate on: Isaiah 59:16

Pray these verses: Psalm 5:1-3, Isaiah 66:7-9

Week 2

Pray For The Church Leadership to Return to Prayer

Read: Acts 4:13-31

Meditate on: Ezekiel 22:30

Pray these verses: Joel 2:12-21, Ephesians 6:18

Week 3

Pray For America To Return To God, His Rule And His Precepts

Read: Psalm 33:4-12, Proverbs 29:2

Meditate on: Proverbs 14:34

Pray these verses: Psalm 9:7-10, 15-20

Week 4

Pray For The Watchmen To Get Back On The Wall

Read: Isaiah 62:6-7, Ezekiel 33:1-7

Meditate on: Isaiah 58:1

Pray these verses: Daniel 9:3-6, Acts 6:4

Example of corporate prayer for Month One, Week One

Pray For The Intercessors To Return To A Life of Prayer

Read: Exodus 32:9-14

Meditate on: Isaiah 59:16

Pray these verses: Psalm 5:1-3, Isaiah 66:7-9

RETURN TO PRAYER

> **Instructions For The Prayer Leader:**
>
> The prayer leader should begin by reading the introduction followed by the subject for this time of prayer and the opening text (Exodus 32:9-14). He or she may use the following example to prepare the group.
>
> Intercessors are individuals who feel a special burden or call to intervene or plead for others to repent and be saved, delivered out of calamities and receive God's mercy instead of his wrath through prayer. Today, we are coming before God to pray because we are burdened in how we and members' of the church have been slack concerning our call and responsibility to intercede. Intercession is the means in which we will use to intervene, plead or petition for those who are in trouble or distress that need divine intervention. Intercessors often travail in prayer. To travail means to undertake a work or task that may be difficult, painful, challenging physically and even mentally to accomplish a desired outcome. In other words, we will continue to cry out to God until Holy Spirit gives us a peace and confidence that God has heard us and is doing something about what we prayed.

The following scriptures reveal to us examples of intercessors. Men like Moses, Daniel and Stephen interceded for others. This is what we can gleam from the following verses about the work of the intercessor.

Psalm 106:23 *"Moses his chosen stood before him in the breach, to turn away his wrath, lest he should destroy them."*

Daniel 9:3-19 *"O Lord, hear; O Lord, forgive; O Lord, hearken and do; defer not, for thine own sake, O my God: for this city and thy people are called by thy name."*

Acts 7:54-59 *"Lord, lay not this sin to their charge."*

> **Instructions For The Prayer Leader:**
>
> The prayer leader may now read the scriptures to be prayed. Invite everyone to gather in a circle, holding hands, to touch and agree as a demonstration of unity. He or she now opens prayer with a brief opening prayer for this time of corporate prayer.

Sample Opening Prayer:

Father, we thank you for everyone gathered here with one mind and one heart to pray. Holy Spirit, we ask you to convict our individual hearts of our sins and purge us so we can become your tools to intercede for others. Holy Spirit, we thank you for guiding and leading us to pray according to the Father's will. Enable us to be the first partakers of returning to intercessory prayer. We acknowledge Satan hates prayer and anyone who will pray to the Father in the name of his son Jesus Christ. Be a shield for us as we engage the enemy, that none of his fiery darts would hinder or distract us in the business at hand. We confess our minds will not wander. No vain imaginations will skew our view of your power to answer our petitions. We will not doubt, nor will our bodies rule us. All things in this room are perfect and conducive to your Spirit working in and through us. We are committed to praying until we spiritually sense your response to our prayers. In Jesus' name, amen.

> **Instructions For The Prayer Leader:**
>
> The prayer leader will call on the first person who God has impressed upon them to pray. The leader will give them an area in which to pray based upon the scriptures. Only that person is to pray. Everyone else in the circle should agree with the person who is praying. No one should be louder than the person praying. If for any reason the prayer is drifting off course, the leader may interrupt and redirect everyone back on course.
>
> The leader will now instruct him or her to pray for Christians who know that they are called to the ministry of intercession to make time to intercede (see Joel 1:13).

Sample Prayer:

Father, we come in the name of your son Jesus Christ to make our petitions. You have instructed us that if we ask anything according to your will, you will hear us. We no longer want you to wonder why there is no intercessor when you have given us this ministry to pray always for all men and for every situation. We take authority against Satan and all of his workers who work diligently and faithfully against your servant's effectiveness in spending set time, long hours, or all night before your altar in prayer. Let the intercessors gird up their mind and be focused on the fact that you are the only answer for all that ails our church, nation, family and neighbors. Let their hearts be burdened and their eyes filled with tears when they see the devastation of sin in the lives of the people around them. Stir them to take immediate action and fall on their knees or go in their secret closets or gather with others to weep and mourn for the lost, the backslider and those ensnared by the wickedness of Satan. Help them to clear their schedules so that they no longer let the cares of this life blind them to their real mission. Cause them to cry out to you as if they cannot be denied. In Jesus' name we ask all these things, amen.

> **Instructions For The Prayer Leader:**
>
> The leader will now call another person in group by name and instruct him or her to pray that the hindrances that Satan uses against the intercessors become null and void as they return to prayer.

Sample Prayer:

Father, I thank you that you have given us authority over all the powers of the enemy and that nothing shall in any wise harm or hinder prayer from being made by your people. You have quickened us and saved us by your grace that we should have the same mind as your son Jesus, who prayed at all times for all things in all places. Let the intercessors that you have anointed in this hour to pray, take by force, possess with all boldness, and wrestle against principalities, powers, the rulers of darkness and against spiritual wickedness in high places. We ask that you give the intercessors a route of escape from situations that the Devil has created to doubt their calling. Let not the Devil prevail against the righteous by whispering lies in their ears. Bless them to put on their whole armor and allow the helmet of salvation to shield their minds from vain imaginations and thoughts of failure. Father, we ask that any distraction of noises, phones ringing, and discomfort of aches or pain, weariness or tiredness in the body will not overwhelm the intercessors from their holy calling. For Zion's sake let them not be silent or intimidated by the enemy. Let all of Satan's plans be of none effect against the intercessors. Grant unto the prayer warriors surpassing victory over all the wiles of the enemy that your will and purposes be accomplished during their time of intercession. In Jesus' name we pray, amen.

> **Instructions For The Prayer Leader:**
>
> The leader will now call another person in the group by name and instruct him or her to pray for the intercessors to return to weeping and mourning over the sins of Christians (see Joel 2:17).

Sample Prayer:

Father, in the name of Jesus Christ of Nazareth, we thank you that we can gather together in this holy assembly for prayer. We have done wickedly, have rebelled, departed from your precepts, ignored the scriptures, and disobeyed your commandment that men ought always to pray. Burden our hearts with the dismal condition of our church. We see the godly perishing, and righteous people are almost nowhere to be found. We have become so preoccupied with our own needs that we've abandoned a genuine concern for others.

You told us if we ask anything according to your will, you will answer. We ask you to cause your face to shine upon us again, so that the things that hurt and grieve your heart will also hurt and grieve our hearts. Grant the intercessors the same compassionate heart you showed mankind, a love so profound that you sacrificed your Son. Let our hearts be pricked by our sin and the sins of other believers. We do not desire that any man should perish, but that all would come to repentance. Even as the psalmist said that rivers of water ran down his face because men have not kept the laws of God, let it be so with us. We have sinned and fallen short of your glory each time we lean on our own understanding and do not pray.

Let your Spirit enable us to see beyond outward appearances of acceptability to God, so we may align ourselves with Holy Scripture. Give us compassion for others who are bound by the Devil, that we may stand in the gap on their behalf. As we examine our own selves, cause us to rend our hearts and not our garments. Spare your people, Lord. Heal our backsliding and renew a right Spirit within us. Against you only have we sinned by not praying and crying out for your divine mercy. In your wrath remember mercy. Be merciful unto us and hear our cry. Father, if you would mark iniquity, no man could stand. Forgive us for becoming slack in our duty and responsibility as the salt of the earth to pray. Help us return to you, to redeem the time and to seek your face early in the morning. In the name of Jesus, amen.

> **Instructions For The Prayer Leader:**
>
> The prayer leader now closes out the prayer with thanksgiving (see Philippians 4:6) by faith that God will reward and give answers to meet the prayer request (see Hebrews 11:6).

Sample Closeout Prayer:

Father, we thank you that you hear us always. We are grateful that you have shown us mercy and given us another opportunity to return to you in prayer. We are confident that the prayers of righteous men and women, through faith, will avail much. With great anticipation, we expect to see our prayers fulfilled as many sons and daughters return to a lifestyle of prayer and intercession. Thank you, Lord, through our prayers, many who the Devil had retired from praying are putting their hand back on the plow to push through the Devil's lies and pray. We rejoice because your search for a man or woman to stand in the gap and pray is over. They have heard the clarion call and are returning to duty. Thank you, Lord, the intercessors are travailing in prayer, and many are being brought forth to delight in prayer. Thank you for good success tonight/today. Let what you have stirred up in us remain in us. We confess we are no longer lukewarm, but hot, fervent and excited to pray. We bless and praise the living God forever and ever in Jesus' name, amen.

These prayers were based on the following scriptures:

Daniel 9:5

John 15:7

Ephesians 6:12

Psalm 119:136

RETURN TO PRAYER

Romans 3:23

Psalm 12:1

Joel 2:17

Psalm 130:3

Psalm 51:4

Habakkuk 2:2

MONTH 2

SEEK TO GO A LITTLE FARTHER IN YOUR PRAYER RELATIONSHIP

"I press toward the mark for the prize of the high calling of God in Christ Jesus" (Philippians 3:14).

Currently, the lack of prioritizing prayer to God has resulted in a spiritual famine among Christians. We seek everything and everyone first and use God as a last option. Intimacy with God is directly proportional to our pursuit of him. Christians fall into three categories in their intimacy with Christ. Some have an outer-court relationship with Jesus whereby they only seek him in prayer because of an emergency. Others have an inner-court relationship. Though they pray, they put limitations on how much of themselves they will surrender to Jesus. Then there is a smaller group of Christians, like Isaiah the prophet, who seek to venture into the holy of holies through intercessory prayer. The holy place is the place of full surrender, not my will but thy will be done. God is inviting us to abandon our will, preferences and pursuits to go a little farther in prayer to seek his plans. Our will must crumble until we surrender, like Jesus, and say yes to the Father. The Bible recounts many Christians who went a little farther. The disciples who gathered in the upper room went a little further. Stephen, apostle Paul, Barnabas, Aquila & Priscilla, and Epaphroditus all went a little farther in prayer. As a result, their prayers achieved much, the church grew, they stopped the Devil's work, and miracles abounded. These days are not gone; any Christian that will seek first the kingdom of God through intercessory prayer and enter the holy place will reap abundant blessings.

Week 1

Pray For Christians To Seek God And Examine Their Prayer Relationship With Christ

Read: Daniel 9:3-10

Meditate on: 2 Corinthians 13:5

Pray these verses: Jeremiah 29:12-13, Luke 18:1

Week 2

Pray For Those In The Outer Court To Seek To Go A Little Farther & Enter The Inner Courts

Read: Luke 19:1-10

Meditate on: Matthew 6:33

Pray these verses: Philippians 3:13-16

Week 3

Pray For Christians In The Inner Court To Seek To Go A Little Farther And Enter The Most Holy Place

Read: Matthew 26:36-46

Meditate on: Galatians 2:20

Pray these verses: James 5:16, 1 Thessalonians 5:17

Week 4

Pray For Christians In The Most Holy Place To Remain Surrendered To Christ

Read: John 15:1-11

Meditate on: James 4:7

Pray these verses: 2 Timothy 4:7, 1 Corinthians 15:57-58

Here is an example of corporate prayer for Month Two, Week Two:

Pray For Christians In The Outer Court To Seek To Go A Littler Farther And Enter The Inner Court

Read: Luke 19:1-10

Meditate on: Matthew 6:33

Pray these verses: Philippians 3:13-16

> **Instructions For The Prayer Leader:**
>
> The prayer leader should begin by reading the introduction followed by the subject for this time of prayer and the opening text (Luke 19:1-10). He or she may follow by defining key words from the introduction and share the goals for this prayer.
>
> The emphasis for this month's corporate prayer is, *Seek To Go A Little Farther In Your Prayer Relationship*. As a reminder, to seek means to look for with an intent to find, secure or receive the object that is being looked for. We are gathered to intercede for those who desire and need to change their distant relationship with Christ to a more intimate and committed relationship. (Our text reminds us of the tabernacle of Moses. There was an Outer Court where most of the people gathered to bring their animal sacrifices to the priest. The Inner Court was only entered by the priest who burned incense to worship God. The Most Holy Place represents the presence of God. It is where the Ark of the Covenant was positioned). Our time of prayer will require us to go a little farther than we may be use to in prayer. That means we will not rush our prayer, we will continue to cry out to God until we sense that change is taking place in those whom we are praying for.
>
> The prayer leader may now read the scriptures to be prayed (Luke 19:1-10). Invite everyone to gather in a circle, holding hands, to touch and agree as a demonstration of unity. He or she now opens prayer with a brief covering prayer for this time of corporate prayer.

Sample Opening Prayer:

Father, we thank you for the privilege of coming together to pray for others. We boldly come to the throne of grace in unity to plead and petition you for a supernatural move in the lives of your children. Holy Spirit, we invite you to reveal the Father's heart, mind and plans as we pray. Help us stand on the written word and wage a good warfare against all that is evil. By faith, we put on our whole armour and stand against the wiles of the devil. His efforts to distract us from our prayer assignment will not prevail. Our thoughts will not drift; we will maintain our focus, and pray until a spiritual breakthrough occurs. Have your way and do your good pleasure in us. In Jesus' name, Amen.

> **Instructions For The Prayer Leader:**
>
> The prayer leader will call on the first person who God has impressed upon them to pray. The leader will give them an area in which to pray based upon the scriptures. Only that person is to pray. Everyone else in the circle agrees with him or her. No one should be louder than the person praying. If for any reason the prayer is drifting off course, the leader may interrupt and redirect everyone back on course.
> The leader will instruct him or her to please pray for Christians to go a little farther by forgetting their past distractions (failures) (Philippians 3:13).

Sample Prayer:

Father, we thank you for your love for us. We are thankful for this opportunity to pray for others. May you pour out your mercy on those Christians who have abandoned you to pursue wealth, status, and success. Bring them to a place where they become tired of being lovers of themselves. Deliver them from the familiar spirits that once led them astray. We pray for these precious ones to escape the snare of the devil. Jesus has given them authority to exercise his name against Satan. Enable them to forget the things in their past that once blinded them. May they confess your word and abide in their new identity. Yesterday is gone; today is a new day with new mercies and victories for them to experience.

Father, you do not condemn those who are in Christ who have strayed. Though they may have fallen many times, you are still upholding them in your arms. Take them through the outer court and into the inner court. Through your Spirit, guide them toward a more meaningful relationship with you. May they see the path of life that you would like them to follow. Help them abandon their insecurities and cause them to know you have placed their past sins as far as the east is to the west. You are faithful and have promised not to turn a deaf ear when they call upon you. Stir their confidence to know that better days are ahead. Your plans toward them are not evil, but for peace and to give them an expected end. Thank you for giving them your wisdom to reach forth and grab hold of eternal life. By faith, they shall look to the hill called Calvary and receive surpassing strength and victory to press towards the mark of the high calling. In Jesus' name, amen.

> **Instructions For The Prayer Leader:**
>
> The leader will now call another person in group by name and instruct him or her to pray for Christians to press to go a little farther in their relationship with Christ (based on Philippians 3:14).

Sample Prayer:

Father, our hearts rejoice for this opportunity to come and pray for our brothers and sisters who are in the outer courts. May they desire more than the status quo of just saying they are Christians. Even as the deer panth for the water brooks, bless them to hunger and thirst for your presence. Though some have gotten weary in well-doing and have allowed their commitment to become lukewarm, may the fire from your Spirit ignite them to run to you. We pray for them to press on, go against their feelings and pursue you with all that is within them. Stir up a longing within them to desire a greater fellowship with you. Let all the obstacles, hindrances and distractions be of no effect against your daily invitation to come and dine with you. Even as your eyes are upon them, let their eyes focus on you. Let them not remain content with their current relationship with you.

Father, we thank you for stirring a desire in your children to cry daily for more of your presence. Show them great and mighty things that they know not of. Let your wisdom guide them out of their rituals and routines. Your people are more than conquerors. The greater one lives within them. Through Christ they can press through and do the things that please you.

Father, you have set an open door before your children. Enable them to walk out of the old and into the inner courts of blessings and favor. You have promised not to withhold any good thing from those who seek you. It is your good pleasure to give them the kingdom. We confess that Christians are anointed to reach forth and grab hold of the things you have set before them. They have the victory. In the name of Jesus, amen.

Instructions For The Prayer Leader:

The leader will call another person by name to pray for Christians to have the mind of Christ to leave their comfort zone and enter into the inner court (Philippians 3:15-16).

Sample Prayer:

Thank you, Lord, for another opportunity to join with others to pray for a right mind in your people who are choosing to enter the inner courts. Let the same mind that was in Christ be in them. As it was Christ lifestyle to commune with you, allow them to return to communing with you. Bless your children to think on the things that are true, honest, just, pure, lovely and of a good report. Father, we pray for their thoughts to be governed by things above more than the things of the world. We take authority over all the works of the Devil in the minds of those who are pursuing greater things in you. Spirits of fear are bound and can no longer hinder your children or keep them in their comfort zone.

As they draw near to you, may they be transformed by the renewing of their minds. Give them a moldable heart that cultivates right thoughts concerning what you want them to do. Those who are hungry for more of you will resist the crowds that follow the wide path and seek the narrow road that leads to life and it more abundantly. Quicken them to continue in your word and seek first your kingdom. By your power, cause them to die to the flesh and their old thoughts. They are more than conquerors. Bless them to shake the dust off their feet and enter the new adventure that you have set before them.

Because the Spirit of God leads them, may they follow in Christ's footsteps and go a little farther to hear your instructions. Allow your still, small voice to be louder than all the other distracting voices. We give God thanks that every plot or scheme of the wicked one is defeated and victory is ours. In Jesus' name, amen.

> **Instructions For The Prayer Leader:**
>
> Prayer leader closes out prayer with thanksgiving (see Philippians 4:6) by faith that God will reward and give answers to meet the prayer request (see Hebrews 11:6).

Sample Closeout Prayer:

Father, we're overflowing with thankfulness for the opportunity to approach your throne of grace with our petitions. Thank you for this opportunity to pray. By faith, we believe our prayers have translated those who were in the outer court into the inner court. We rejoice in their becoming more sensitive to the wooing of your Spirit to move forward in their relationship with you. As the sheep of your pasture, they are now tuned in to hearing the voice of their Shepherd. They will never be the same. You have stirred up a new desire in them to allow you to lead them to green pastures. Though heaven and earth may pass away, we trust you to perform your word in their lives. Your word is a lamp to their feet, will not return void, and will accomplish every intent of your heart. Thank you for granting our petition. In Jesus' name, amen.

These prayers were based on the following scriptures:

Micah 7:19

Romans 8:1

Jeremiah 29:11

Psalm 42:1

Galatians 6:9

Jeremiah 33:3

Roman 8:37

Philippians 2:5

Colossians 3:1

Matthew 7:13-14

Romans 12:1-2

Philippians 6:8, Philippians 1:21

MONTH 3

HUMBLE YOURSELF

"If my people, which are called by my name, shall humble themselves, and pray, and seek my face, and turn from their wicked ways; then will I hear from heaven, and will forgive their sin, and will heal their land" (2 Chronicles 7:14).

Not only is our nation in moral and spiritual decay, but the church is following hard on the heels of the world. The church has lost its distinction between the holy and the unholy, the clean and the unclean. The gold or pure things of God have been removed out of the sanctuary and copper or an impure mixture has been brought in. Though gold and copper look similar, their components, makeup and composition are different. The church appears irrelevant to the sinner, hypocritical to the skeptic and outdated to the new agers. Many view the church as dead and its God as dead. God is not dead, and the church is not dead! The church is just ripe for a revival. Revival is a renewed interest in spiritual things or resurrection of one who was spiritually dead back to being a lively stone. This is shown by a hunger for biblical truths, a renewed desire for daily Bible reading, a restored and cultivated prayer/communication with our heavenly Father, a deep conviction to prioritize God in our lives, and a reawakening to see sinners saved. Therefore, revival is a term for Christians alone. It is the Christians who need to be revived, not the sinner. A revival will not come just because someone with a well-publicized name comes into a city and preaches some services that they call "Revival". Before there is a city revival, there must be a people who are hot, on fire and excited about the things of God. There must be a humbling attitude in those who are part of the local church before we can help others to change their lives. The first prerequisite for revival according to 2 Chronicles 7:14 is humility. In the Greek, tapeinoo is the root word for humble, and it often refers to the idea of abasing oneself to make oneself low considering the greatness and majesty of God. It speaks of choosing to make Christ high and ourselves low out of reverence, respect and dependency.

Week 1

Pray For The Body Of Christ To Humble Themselves And Agree With God That We Need A Revival

Read: Isaiah 5:11-23

Meditate On: 1 Peter 5:6

Pray these verses: Daniel 9:5-6, 17-19, James 4:6

Week 2

Pray For Christians To Humble Themselves And Pray For A Revival To Begin In Them

Read: 2 Timothy 3:1-7

Meditate on: Psalm 85:6

Pray these verses: James 4:6-10

Week 3

Pray For The Clergy To Humble Themselves, Preach and Live The Scriptures

Read: 1 Corinthians 9:16-27

Meditate On: Matthew 23:12

Pray these verses: Acts 20:19-21, 27-28

Week:4

Pray For The False Prophets To Repent For Leading God's People Astray And Humbly Confess Their Sin

Read: 2 Peter 2:2:1, 2 Peter 2:12-22

Meditate On: Colossians 4:6

Pray these verses: Psalm 51:1-4, Ephesians 4:25

Here is an example of corporate prayer for Month Three, Week Three:

Pray For The Clergy To Humble Themself, Preach and Live The Scriptures

> **Instructions For The Prayer Leader:**
>
> The prayer leader should begin by reading the introduction followed by the subject for this time of prayer and the opening text of 1 Corinthians 9:16-27. He or she may follow up by defining key words from the introduction and share the goals for this prayer.
>
> The emphasis in this month's corporate prayer is on humbling yourself. Humility often refers to the idea of abasing oneself and of making oneself low considering the greatness and majesty of God. It also speaks of a willingness to choose to make Christ high and ourselves low out of reverence, respect and dependency. This prayer is for the clergy to humble themselves, preach the Scriptures, and live by them. Now the leader will read the following scriptures for this time of prayer (Acts 20:19-21, 27-28). Invite everyone to gather in a circle, joining hands, to touch and agree as a demonstration of unity.
>
> The leader now opens prayer with a brief opening prayer for this time of corporate prayer.

Sample Opening Prayer:

> Father, we come before you with gratitude that you have chosen to use us to pray for the clergy. Each person who is in this circle has a heartfelt concern for church leaders. We too have been slack in not humbling ourselves to do your will. We lay down our own shortcomings and choose to depend upon your Holy Spirit to lead us as we pray for the clergy to humble themselves. May you fill our mouths with the words you would have us pray. Thank you for hearing us always and sending the answers to our petitions. In Jesus' name, amen.

> **Instructions For The Prayer Leader:**
>
> The prayer leader will call on the first person who God has impressed upon him or her to pray. The leader will give them an area in which to pray based upon the scriptures. Only that person is to pray. Everyone else in the circle agrees with him or her. No one should be louder than the person praying. If for any reason the prayer is drifting off course, the leader may interrupt and redirect everyone back on course.
>
> The leader will now instruct him or her to pray for pastors, ministers, deacons and others who make up the clergy to humble themself and serve God's people.

Sample Prayer:

Our Father, we gather to hallow your great name and to ask for mercy from you. Many of our clergy have forgotten that they are to be servants and follow in Jesus' footsteps. Some have sought to be great without living a life of servitude, and others despise the very thought that they should serve the congregation. May the Spirit renew their minds so that they humble themselves. In your lovingkindness, turn their hearts towards obedience to your Spirit. May the eyes of their understanding be enlightened with the knowledge of why you have called each of them.

Father, you resist the proud and give grace unto the humble. Touch our pastors and ministers to allow your grace to be manifested in their lives. May our clergy cast down every vain imagination and high thought the enemy suggests. Give them victory over the old mindset, old attitudes and selfish demeanor. Stir up a pure heart in them to delight to do your will and to serve you daily. Remind them that you will not forget their labor of love towards your people. As they serve, lift them up. We thank you that you will not withhold any good thing from those who serve you faithfully by feeding the sheep. In Jesus' name, amen.

> **Instructions For The Prayer Leader**
>
> The leader will then call another person by name to pray for the clergy to preach the Gospel freely and not exploit God's people for personal financial gain.

Sample Prayer:

O' God, hear us from heaven as we cry out to you. The number of righteous preachers seems to decrease, and the hirelings seem to be on the rise. They have become lovers of money more than lovers of God. The enemy has been using money to get some of the clergy to preach another gospel. Though many souls are desiring to hear a word of truth, they are only hearing messages that entertain, tantalize and feed their flesh. Father, we ask you to deliver those who only preach for personal profit to return to you with their whole heart. Cause them to rend their hearts and not their fancy garments. Show them the error of their ways and give them a route of escape. Even as the prodigal son came home, cause these prodigal preachers to come home desiring only to be a servant in your house.

We pray for the remnant of clergy who preach the word in season and out of season to continue to humble themselves and do your bidding. May the words they speak from the throne of grace refresh the weary and water the thirsty. Let them hold nothing back that would be profitable to cause the people to grow. Anoint them to sow seeds of truth so that many people would hear and become free. Be gracious unto them and supply their every need. When temptation arises, bless them to stand firm on your promises. Quickened them to boldly declare that they do not live by money alone, but by every word of God.

Thank you for sparing those clergy deceived into thinking your house was a gambling hall or their personal bank. We appreciate you, Father, for giving them another chance to do your will. By faith, we believe you will renew a right spirit in our clergy that will cause them to preach the whole counsel of God with humility. In Jesus' name, amen.

> **Instructions For The Prayer Leader**
>
> The leader will then call another person by name to pray for the clergy to humbly live what they teach and preach.

Sample Prayer:

Great is the Lord, and greatly to be praised. Father, we count it a joy to come before the throne of grace to seek help in our time of need. We are troubled that many of our clergy are living double lives. They preach one thing and live a different life. Their double lives cause their families to suffer, confuse the congregation, and alienate the communities they serve from seeking you. Sin has become fashionable and second nature to them. Only you, our God, can deliver them from their blindness and ignorance. We beseech you to arrest their attention during their double-mindedness. We know there is nothing too hard for you. You can write on the walls of their church and cause them to bow their knees in repentance. Visit them, Lord.

Father, it is not your desire to destroy the clergy who have a form of godliness and yet deny your power. Stir them through your Holy Spirit to run the race that is set before them. Enable them to live by faith in the Son of God and not by sight. Help them clear their schedules, examine themselves and draw near to you. Teach them the ways of your precept, that their lives do not cause others to stumble. May they come to a place of godly sorrow and put away the fictitious Bible that they have embraced. As they exalt your greatness over their lives, allow them to study your word in reverence and holy awe. Cleanse them as they study and eat of the word of life. Remind them you bought them and fashioned them with your own hands to serve your purposes. Quickened them to separate themselves from the world and come out from among them. Lavish your grace upon them as they return to a place of humility.

By faith, we see the clergy living a life of consecration and dedication to you. They are no longer straddling the fence. They are making their calling and election sure. Thank you for bringing them out of bondage with your strong arm. Be it unto us according to our faith in your promises. In Jesus' name, amen.

> **Instructions For The Prayer Leader:**
>
> The prayer leader closes out the prayer with thanksgiving (see Philippians 4:6) by faith that God will reward and give answers to meet the prayer request (see Hebrews 11:6).

Sample Closeout Prayer:

Father, you are the only one who can answer our prayers. Therefore, it is a privilege that we can come together in unity and offer our prayers for the clergy. By faith, we believe the Holy Spirit led us to pray what was on your heart. We are in anticipation and filled with excitement about what you are going to do with these prayers. We rejoice the clergy will not be the same. Humility will be their inward passion and outward garment. They will approach all things with submission and total dependency on you. Their lives will testify that they are your humble servants. Thank you for answering our prayers. In Jesus' name, amen.

These prayers were based on the following scriptures:

Ephesians 4:23

Ephesians 1:18

2 Corinthians 10:5

Joel 2:13

Philippians 4:19

Matthew 4:4

Galatians 2:20

2 Corinthians 6:17

Acts 20:19-21, 27-28

James 4:6-7

MONTH 4

INTERNALIZE GOD'S WORD

"This book of the law shall not depart out of thy mouth; but thou shalt meditate therein day and night, that thou mayest observe to do according to all that is written therein: for then thou shalt make thy way prosperous, and then thou shalt have good success" (Joshua 1:8).

Christianity has become something very different from when the church was born in the book of Acts. Worldly fads and fashions, carnal church services, entertainment-guided worship, and unregenerated men resembling the priesthood of God often overrun the church today. Perverted scripture translations have corrupted all that should be holy. Rituals of going to church, the use of religious clichés, wearing costly garments and an outward appearance of piety weaken and trample the Gospel message of the word becoming flesh and dwelling amongst us and in us. God's word must take priority in our lives in order for us to bear Christian fruit. The blessings of a renewed mind are available to us if we meet God's condition to know him. A people who know (internalize) their God will do great exploits. Internalizing Christ's word into our daily lives molds us into people who please the Father. When we internalize Christ, his values will become our values, his meat will become our meat, his ways will become our ways, and his mind will become our mind. All that is consistent with the character of Jesus Christ through the scriptures, Bible teaching and revelations from the Holy Spirit will become a part of our make-up. Only then will it be possible for you and I to say; I am a new creature, old things are passed away (see 2 Corinthians 5:17), the same mind that was in Christ is in me also (see Philippians 2:5) and Christ has left me an example. Therefore, I follow in his footstep (see 1 Peter 2:21). It is when the world sees Christ internalized in our lives that they will follow us to the Master (see Zechariah 8:23). When Christians internalize Christ, the church will become revived, and sinners will repent and find salvation. There is no good thing that God will withhold from those who let his word richly dwell in them and who live and do the word. Let us intercede in prayer for the renewal of our minds through the internalizing of what God's word says about us.

Week 1

Pray for Christians To Internalize God's Promises And Continue In The Word

Read: Acts 2:38-47

Meditate On: 2 Corinthians 1:20

Pray these verses: John 8:31-32

Week 2

Pray For Pastor's To Internalize The Word And Preach The Whole Counsel Of God

Read: Galatians 6:6-10

Meditate On: 1 Corinthians 9:16

Pray these verses: 2 Timothy 4:1-5

Week 3

Pray For Parents To Internalize The Word And Teach It To Their Children

Read: Deuteronomy 11:18-21

Meditate On: James 1:22

Pray these verses: Joshua 1:8, Proverbs 22:6

Week 4

Pray For Christian Teachers To Internalize The Truth And Teach The Truth

Read: John 15:4-11

Meditate On: Psalm 119:11

Pray these verses: 1 Timothy 4:11-16

Here is an example of corporate prayer for Month Four, Week Four:

Pray For Christian Teachers To Internalize The Truth And Teach The Truth

INTERNALIZE GOD'S WORD

> **Instructions For The Prayer Leader:**
>
> The prayer leader should begin by reading the introduction followed by the subject for this time of prayer and the opening text of First Timothy 4:11-16. He or she may follow up by defining key words from the introduction and share the goals for this prayer.
>
> The emphasis in this month's corporate prayer is Internalizing God's Word. To internalize is to accept, or absorb an idea, opinion or belief so that it becomes a part of your character. Abide means to remain, to stay and to continue in a place. As we stand in the gap for teachers, our goal is to pray that the word of Christ will richly dwell in them, shape their views, and govern their actions. The leader will now read the scriptures that are to be prayed (John 15:4-11). Invite everyone to gather in a circle, holding hands, to touch and agree as we pray for teachers to teach the truth. The leader now opens prayer with a brief opening prayer for this time of corporate prayer.

Sample Opening Prayer:

Father, we thank you for this opportunity to lift our hearts in our hands to you. We gather to share our burden for teachers who are believers in Christ, to internalize your word to aid them in teaching their students. Our concern for the next generation motivates us to stand in the gap and place a hedge around the minds and hearts of those called to teach our children. Bless everyone gathered here to pray led by your Spirit. May we have good success as we pray for these teachers. In Jesus' name, amen.

> **Instructions For The Prayer Leader:**
>
> The prayer leader will call on the first person who God has impressed upon him or her to pray. The leader will give them an area in which to pray based upon the scriptures. Only that person is to pray. Everyone else in the circle agrees with him or her. No one should be louder than the person praying. If for any reason the prayer is drifting off course, the leader may interrupt and redirect everyone back on course. The leader will now instruct him or her to pray for Christian teachers to internalize the gift of teaching that was given to them (1 Timothy 4:12-14).

Sample Prayer:

Heavenly Father, every good and perfect gift comes from you. Teaching is one of those gifts. Forgive us who are gathered in this circle who have been set apart to teach others in formal settings or in our home or community who have ignored using this gift. May those called with a holy calling with the gift to teach hold fast to their profession of faith without wavering when they are challenged to accommodate falsehood. Bless them to remember their holy calling to nurture and develop others through teaching the truth from a Christian world view.

May those that are in Christ, continue to lift up the blood-stained banner. Though many Christians are daily conforming to the world standards in what they teach, allow those appointed by you to teach without compromise. No weapon that is formed against these teachers will prosper. The greater one lives and abides in them. The same mind that was in Christ is in them also. They delight to do your will. As they teach, give them insight, revelation and wisdom according to your Spirit. We believe the truth they share will make the learners free and enable them to grow.

We confess, these teachers will not abandon the truth when opposition arise. They will stand firm in the word with their loins girded by the truth. The eyes of their understanding are enlightened with truth and illuminates their path. Quicken your teachers to cling to the truth and resist every lie. In Jesus' mighty name, amen.

> **Instructions For The Prayer Leader:**
>
> The leader will now call another person by name and instruct him or her to pray for Christian teachers to internalize/abide in Christ as they teach their students (John 15:4-11).

Sample Prayer:

Our God and King, we come to you in the name of Jesus Christ, our Lord and Savior. Let your words abide in the Christian teachers in whatsoever venue they are privileged to teach. Whether secular venues or Christian venues, allow them to be the branch that abides in the vine. May these teachers approve things that are excellent for their students. Anoint them to teach by example, word and deed. We confess they are steadfast, unmovable, always abounding in the work of God and never faltering in their commitment or compromising in what they speak. There yes are yes and their nos are nos.

We pray that these teachers daily seek you as they prepare to teach their classes. Remind them to be more dependent on your Spirit rather on their own abilities, skills, or educational training. Grant them patience to search out the best methods to reach their students in the lessons they are teaching. Quicken them to respond and be dependent on the Holy Spirit. The letter kills, but your Spirit makes what they teach come to life.

Let them reflect their love for Christ in their love for their students. Enable them to hold back nothing that would be profitable for their students. Guide them to teach line upon line and precept upon precept, so that they build a strong foundation in their students using the basic

INTERNALIZE GOD'S WORD

building blocks of the subjects they teach. Let their passion for the subjects they teach stir up a hunger in their students to have a greater interest in learning.

Father, you have made these godly teachers the head and not the tail. No matter their challenges, empower them by your Spirit to remain faithful and true. We confess, they do not walk by sight, by political correctness, or by media influence. Theirs is a walk of faith in the incorruptible word of God. Bless them to bear fruit in the lives of their students long after their students have moved on. Thanks be to God, who gives them the ability to be disciples and examples for Christ. In Jesus' name, amen.

> **Instructions For The Prayer Leader:**
>
> The leader will now call another person by name and instruct him or her to pray for Christian teachers to internalize the truth of God's word and teach it (John 15:4-11).

Sample Prayer:

Father in a day where political correctness dominates our educational system, may your teachers never cease to teach the truth. Allow what they teach to come out of the word they have hidden in their heart. Empower them to uphold the holy scriptures as they teach biology, physical education, history classes and other subjects. Guide the science teachers to draw a clear line that lift up the creation story above all other theories.

May, Christian teachers embrace the truth of your word and remain free through it. According to John 1:1 to know the Word is to know and teach about God. Quicken them to dispense the truth of your word to encourage the students to honor God. All scripture is given by inspiration of God, and is profitable for doctrine, correction, reproof and instructions in righteousness. Bless these teachers to be discerning and use every method to reveal to the students that all things were made by God and for God.

As these teachers give themself to you, may they continually be filled with your Spirit. We bind spirits of fear, stress and worry. Your teachers will not be discouraged by what they hear from the teacher's union or local government officials. Their trust is in the Lord who controls every heart of man and turns it as he chooses. Bless them to be confident that you have called them and equipped them to stand when they are challenged. You are the one who has begun a good work in them and you will fulfill it. In the name of your son the Lord Jesus Christ, Amen.

> **Instructions For The Prayer Leader:**
>
> The prayer leader closes out the prayer with thanksgiving (see Philippians 4:6) by faith that God will reward and give answers to meet the prayer request (see Hebrews 11:6).

Sample Closeout Prayer:

Father, we give thanks to you; these teachers will never be the same. The prayers made by righteous men and women on their behalf avail much in their lives. We confess these teachers are now transformed vessels, renewed in their minds, dependent on your Holy Spirit, and subject to your authority. Freely they have received from you, and freely they are making eternal deposits in the lives of their students. Thank you for the change that is taking place in the children as they are hearing the truth of God's word through these teachers. In Christ we pray, amen.

These prayers were based on the following scriptures:

1 Timothy 4:12-14

John 15:4-11

Philippians 1:10

Romans 8:14

2 Corinthians 3:6

Deuteronomy 28:13

2 Timothy 3:16

2 Corinthians 5:7

Philippians 1:6

MONTH 5

GROW IN GRACE

"But grow in grace, and in the knowledge of our Lord and Saviour Jesus Christ" (2 Peter 3:18).

The apostle Peter admonishes us to, *"beware lest ye also, being led away with the error of the wicked, fall from your own steadfastness"* (2 Peter 3:17-18). Growth is development or improvement toward a goal called maturity or perfection. Growth is a natural part of life. In fact, growth is one sign that something is alive. This is true both in the natural realm and in the spiritual realm. If a church is alive, it should be growing. Likewise, if a person is alive, he or she should be growing. God's word shows he wants more than a few spiritual offspring. He wants his house to be full (see Luke 14:23), none to perish (see 2 Peter 3:9), and he desires to bring many sons to glory (see Hebrews 2:10). Jesus revealed the Father's heart when he instructed the disciples to go into all nations (see Mark16:15), make disciples of all men (see Matthew 28:19) and be his witnesses to the ends of the earth (see Acts 1:8). Therefore, it is our responsibility to position ourselves deliberately by studying God's word, embracing right association and teaching, to grow individually and to grow God's church numerically. Let us pray for ourselves and those in the Body of Christ to grow spiritually.

Week 1

Pray for Christians To Grow In Christ By Repenting Of Their Sin

Read: Romans 6:1-4, Ephesians 1:3-6

Meditate on: Ephesians 2:8

Pray these verses: Psalms 51:1-4, 2 Peter 3:18

Week 2

Pray For Christians To Spiritually Grow In Grace So That They Do Not Become A Stumblingblock To Believers Or Unbelievers

Read: Romans 14:11-19

Meditate on: Ephesians 5:15

Pray these verses: Ephesians 4:22-32, 2 Timothy 2:1

Week 3

Pray For Christian Leaders In The Church To Grow In Grace And Teach Sound Doctrine

Read: 1 Corinthians 2:1-5, Ephesians 3:7-10

Meditate On: 2 Timothy 1:9

Pray these verses: 2 Corinthians 4:5-6, 2 Timothy 4:2-5

Week 4

Pray For Celebrity Christians In Hollywood To Grow In Grace And Avoid Sin

Read: Colossians 3:1-5, 2 Timothy 3:1-5

Meditate on: Proverbs 3:34

Pray these verses: Philippians 3:13-14, Romans 5:20-21

Here is a Sample Corporate Prayer For Month Five, Week One

Week 1

Pray for Christians To Grow In Grace By Repenting Of Their Sin

Read: Romans 6:1-4, Ephesians 1:3-6

Meditate on: Ephesians 2:8

Pray these verses: Psalms 51:1-4, 2 Peter 3:18

GROW IN GRACE

> **Instructions For The Prayer Leader:**
>
> The prayer leader should read the introduction, then the subject and the opening texts, Romans 6:1-4 and Ephesians 1:3-6. Everyone should have pondered the scripture before coming to the prayer meeting. The prayer leader may make brief comments at this time to guide the participant. This is not a preaching occasion, but a time to focus on prayer.
>
> The emphasis in this month's corporate prayer is the keyword, grow. The admonition to grow refers to maturing by studying and listening to God's word with a willingness to take Christ's yoke upon us and learn of him. We cannot overlook the genuine need for repentance, for without it there can be no healthy growth. To repent means to acknowledge sin, turn away from it, proceed in the opposite direction and never go back. Let us acknowledge our sin and the sins of others so that we can pray about the things that hinder us or them from growing in God's grace.
>
> The prayer leader may now read the scriptures to be prayed (Psalms 51:1-4, 1 Thessalonians 4:1-6). Invite everyone to gather in a circle, holding hands, to touch and agree to show unity (Matthew 18:19). The leader now opens with a brief covering prayer for this time of intercessory prayer.

Sample Opening Prayer:

    Lord Jesus, we gather in this place to pray for ourselves and our brethren in Christ, that we would examine ourselves and be repentant of every weight and sin that so easily beset us from growing in your grace. Let every person in this gathering be of the same mind and heart. Help us take off the mask and façade and see ourselves, before a holy God. Let us put every vain, foolish and distracting imagination out of our thoughts and minds. Guide us to concentrate on the purpose we are in this place. Holy Spirit, we invite you to help us pray when we don't know what to pray. We yield our vocal cords, thoughts and body to you. Use us as you choose to pray your heart and mind, that those that were in captivity may be free to grow. Grant us and those for whom we pray a greater sense of your presence so that our prayers may eternally change them. Thank you for good success as we prepare to grow in your grace, in Jesus' name, amen.

> **Instructions For The Prayer Leader:**
>
> The leader will now call the first person who God has impressed upon him or her to pray for those in this gathering to acknowledge his or her sin (Psalm 51:1-4) and repent.

Sample Prayer:

    O' Lord, you know all things, for there is nothing hid from you. If we ascend up into heaven, thou art there, and if we make our bed in hell, you there as well. There is nothing hidden from you. Against you only have we sinned and have done wickedly. Each of us who are gathered here has disobeyed your word to grow in your grace and has not used the tools you have made available for us to grow. We have turned a deaf ear to the men of God who have preached the uncompromising word of truth by your Holy Spirit. Guilt is all over us; we have not read the sacred scriptures that teach us your character and nature. We have followed hirelings who disregard the sheep, we've adopted secular humanistic ideas, cultural relativism, feel-good gospels, and aligned ourselves with worldly values.

Some of us have sought to do what was right in our own sight, ignoring the gift of the Holy Spirit to lead us into all truth. We know you do not hear sinners. We desire you to hear us from heaven and heal our land. So, we ask you, Father, to have mercy upon us according to your lovingkindness. We acknowledge we have sinned and fallen short of your glory. We have not learned Christ and have remained spiritual babies who cannot handle strong meat. For your namesake, pardon our iniquity. Each of us takes this time to ask you to forgive us. Blot out our transgressions and grant us the privilege to grow and mature in spiritual things. We no longer want to handle your word as unskilled servants. Hear us, Lord, and grant us another opportunity to grow in your grace. Through Christ our Lord, amen.

> **Instructions For The Prayer Leader:**
>
> The prayer leader will now call on another person by name to pray for Christians to acknowledge his or her sin (Psalm 51:1-4) and repent for not growing and maturing in Christ.

Sample Prayer:

Father, like King David, there are many believers in our church who have sinned and are covering it up from men. They have sometimes used their position or title to hide their sins. Some are leaders in our church, others serve in various capacities, and there are others who are being observed by some person who wants to know you. They have in secret touched, tasted and handled the unclean thing. Whether the unclean thing was a lie, thievery, envy, an evil thought, procrastination, rejecting truth or the defilement of their temples, it is all sin to you.

Father, visit your children, let them see the handwriting upon the wall or send a messenger to them to expose their sin. Nathan the prophet was not seeking to destroy King David, but to show him the errors of his ways and to bring him to a place of conviction so he could grow in you. We ask you to use vessels like the prophet Nathan, who love you and the brethren so much that they will speak the truth in love. Lord, send your angels to block your disciples, who have temporarily forgotten your holiness and are on the verge of becoming a stumbling block. Let not those who once honored you perish in their sin. Father, in your wrath remember mercy.

GROW IN GRACE

We plead for your divine intervention to interrupt their comings and goings, that they may be enlightened with truth. Only you can take the taste and smell of sin out of their mouths and nostrils. We ask you to help them set their eyes on you and take them off pornography and all things that would defile them. We ask for divine intervention in the night hours when they would walk the streets looking for a sexual or drug fix. Let not their feet run to do evil, or their ears become a garbage box to listen to filthy conversation, or their mouths curse instead of bless. We ask you to calm the raging storms of angry in them that lead them to physically abuse their spouses, children and fellow believers.

We take authority over every familiar spirit and every unloving spirit that would seek to keep them in denial and on a path of destruction. Give them the courage to come clean with you. Father, you said, a broken and a contrite heart you will not despise. Pour your great mercy into their lives. Renew in these precious vessels a new spirit and create in them a clean heart. In the merciful name of Jesus, amen.

> **Instructions For The Prayer Leader:**
>
> The leader will now call another person by name and instruct him or her to pray for Christians to be restored in their relationship with Christ after they repent.

Sample Prayer:

Father, we ask you in the name of Jesus Christ to restore unto those who had embraced sin for a season and are now repentant to right fellowship with you. Let them recognize that sin is exceedingly sinful so that they will not look back. Because they have confessed their sin to you, manifest your faithfulness and forgive them. Blot out their transgressions and cast their sins into the sea of forgetfulness. As you have forgiven them, enable them to forgive themselves. We ask you to undergird them to accept the consequences of their sin. For those who need to step down from their positions, grant them the grace to abandon their image and spend time with you. Let them be more concerned with what you think than what men might say. Reignite in them a desire to be a God-chaser and a God-pleaser more than a man-pleaser. Guide them and direct them so that they do not walk by sight but by faith.

Even as the deer pants after the water brooks, quicken them to hunger and thirst for you. Help them go past the worldly crowds and others who only have a form of godliness and allow your word to purge them. Let their associations and friendships be with strong Bible-believing Christians who will hold them accountable. Order their steps in your word, that they may seek pastors after your own heart, who will be an example for them and will feed them with knowledge and understanding. Surround them with such things as they have need of so that they will continue to come out from among them and separate themselves from the old man. Enable them to nurture the new man who is recreated in righteousness and true holiness. We thank you, Father, for hearing us always and granting us the petitions of our hearts. We believe, and therefore we receive the answers to our petitions. In Jesus's name, amen!

> **Instructions For The Prayer Leader:**
>
> The leader will now call another person by name and instruct him or her to pray for Christians to demonstrate that they are growing in Christ.

Father, we are so privileged to call on your name and bring our petitions to you. We beseech you with the help of your Holy Spirit to aid fellow Christians to walk and live daily in such a way others will know you have transformed them. By your mercy and grace, crucify their old man. Moses' encounter with you caused his face to shine; likewise, let the faces of your children shine with the glory of your presence. Cause those who look on them to know that they have taken your yoke upon them. Allow them to hear sound doctrine and apply it to their lives. Bless them to be doers of the word and not hearers only. Let it be clear that their yeas are yeas and their nays are nays. Let their words be seasoned with salt and spoken with grace, to glorify God.

Quicken them to be more concerned about the needs of others, so much so that they mind the things of others more than their own things. Anoint them to present themselves as a living sacrifice, holy and acceptable unto you. Bless them not to straddle the fence; are indecisive, or waver in their Christian walk. In times past where they would lash out at others in retaliation for a perceived offense, let them be quick to forgive, turning the other cheek, and have compassion on others. Clothe them with a childlike spirit so that they no longer exhibit a selfish, prideful, stubborn or worldly spirit. Enable these growing Christians to walk in the newness of life in word and deed. As they mature, guide them to rely on your Spirit so that the saints are edified and sinners are reconciled. May they internalize your character in such a way that others only see the fruit of the Spirit in their lives. Thank you, Lord, that your servants are growing in grace and daily desiring the sincere milk of the word. In Jesus' name, amen.

> **Prayer Leader: Closes out prayer**
>
> The prayer leader closes out the prayer with thanksgiving (see Philippians 4:6) by faith that God will reward and give answers to meet the prayer request (see Hebrews 11:6).

Sample Closeout Prayer:

Father, you said if we ask anything according to your will; you hear us and will grant us the petitions of our heart. We thank you for your desire to see your children grow in your grace. Therefore, we are confident that we have our petition. We appreciate your having listened to our supplications. We rejoice that our request is a light thing for you. There is nothing too hard or difficult for you to do. You are the God of all flesh. You created all things in heaven and on earth, visible and invisible, whether they are thrones or dominions or principalities or powers: all things are subject to you. Knowing you control everything comforts us. It is your good pleasure to give us the kingdom. We can therefore trust you to instruct, guide and direct us to grow in a healthy and beneficial way that will glorify you and bless us. So, we thank you for a teachable spirit and a willingness in your people to grow in your grace. Thank you for forgiving our sins. We confess we have left our comfort zone and are pressing into obedience to your word. We offer our hearts in our hands that you may lead us by still waters and into green pastures as we embark on an exciting journey of growth and maturity. Do all these things for your glory in Jesus' name, amen.

These prayers were based on the following scriptures:

Psalm 139:8

1 John 5:15

Ephesians 4:15

Psalm 42:1

1 Thessalonians 4:4

Psalm 51:1- 4, 9, 10, 17

J ohn 10:12

2 Peter 3:18

Roman 3:23

Romans 6:4-6

James 1:22

Colossians 4:6

Romans 12:1

2 Corinthians 4:2

Proverbs 1:16

Hebrews 12:1

James 4:8

2 Corinthians 5:17

2 Timothy 3:5

Jeremiah 3:15

Colossians 1:16

2 Corinthians 6:17

Ephesians 4:24

MONTH 6

BE BIBLICALLY TRANSFORMED

"And be renewed in the spirit of your mind; And that ye put on the new man, which after God is created in righteousness and true holiness" (Ephesians 4:23-24).

    We all have something about ourselves that we would like to change. Many self-help books line our shelves, and motivational speakers peddle their formula of how to be the best you. The change most people pursue is an outward change. Some seek to undergo a remodeling type of change as if they were a building under construction, and others pursue a behavioral change (no more smoking, no more alcohol). Neither of these external changes will produce an eternal change. All change is not good if it ignores the word of God. The Holy Scriptures do not teach about an outward change; it only speak of an inward change. This kind of change is called transformation, and it is solely the work of the Holy Spirit through the word of God. In this hour, the Holy Spirit is reminding us of the need to experience Biblical transformation. In the Epistle to the Romans, the apostle Paul reminds the Romans and us how to be biblically transformed, *"And be not conformed to this world: but be ye transformed by the renewing of your mind, that ye may prove what is that good, and acceptable, and perfect, will of God"* (Romans 12:2). Biblical transformation is an inward change that causes us to glorify God and not ourselves, edify other Christians and live a life that convicts and reconciles sinners. Let us pray to be biblically transformed by the renewing of our minds.

Week 1

Pray For Christians To Be Biblically Transformed As They Die To Self

Read: Matthew 16:24-26

Meditate on: Romans 12:2

Pray these verses: Colossians 3:1-4, Galatians 2:20

Week 2

Pray For Pastors & Ministers of The Gospel To Live A Biblically Transformed Life That Preach The Truth

Read: Jeremiah 5:26-31, Jeremiah 10:21

Meditate on: 1 Peter 4:17

Pray these verses: 1 Corinthians 2:1-5, 2 Corinthians 4:5

Week 3

Pray For Persecuted Christians In The Workplace To Live A Biblically Transformed Life That Convicts And Reconcile Sinners

Read: Matthew 5:43-48

Meditate on: 1 Corinthians 2:16

Pray these verses: Philippians 2:13-16

Week 4

Pray For Christian Fathers To Live A Biblically Transformed Life That Teaches Their Children To Glorify God

Read: 1Timothy 1:1-4, 2 Timothy 1:2-4

Meditate on: Romans 12:2

Pray these verses: Proverbs 13:22a, 22:6, Ephesians 6:4, 1 Corinthians 11:1

Here is an example of corporate prayer for Month 6, Week 2

Pray For Pastors & Ministers of The Gospel To Live A Biblically Transformed Life That Preach The Truth

BE BIBLICALLY TRANSFORMED

> **Instructions For The Prayer Leader:**
>
> The prayer leader should begin by reading the introduction followed by the subject for this time of prayer and the opening text (Jeremiah 5:26-31 and Jeremiah 10:21). He or she may follow by defining Biblical transformation.
>
> The emphasis in this month's corporate prayer is biblical transformation. Biblical transformation is an inside work by the Holy Spirit who influences a person, renews their mind, and empowers them to resist the world. We have all seen headlines of prominent pastors and ministers who have fallen from grace, so to speak, and others who have merchandised the gospel to line their own pockets. Without a return to the scriptures and submission to the Holy Spirit, these headlines will only multiply. Our task is to pray for those who teach or preach the gospel to undergo an internal change that will enable them to be lights and epistles for Christ, not sources of stumbling.
>
> The prayer leader may now read the scriptures to be prayed (1 Corinthians 2:1-5 and 2 Corinthians 4:5) and invite everyone to gather in a circle, holding hands, to touch and agree as a demonstration of unity.
>
> Prayer leader opens prayer with a brief covering prayer for this time of corporate prayer.

Sample Opening Prayer:

Blessed be the name of the Lord. The name of the Lord is a strong tower. The righteous run into it, and are saved. Father, we take this opportunity to run to you with our prayers. We know it pleases you we should offer prayers and stand in the gap for others. We come to call upon your name for those who minister the Gospel. May each intercessor gathered here fix his or her focus on the task at hand. We are protected and sheltered under your wings to carry out our divine assignment. Therefore, I confess no weapon formed against our time of prayer will prosper. Our mission is clear, our purpose defined, and we submit our will to your will. Pray through us your plans and purposes for your pastors and ministers who teach the word in the church. By faith, we trust you to hear our prayers and manifest the answers to our petitions. In Christ, our Sovereign King, we pray, amen.

> **Instructions For The Prayer Leader:**
>
> The prayer leader will call on the first person who God has impressed upon him or her to pray for pastors and ministers who have misused their call to teach the gospel to return to the potters' house (based on Jeremiah 10:21).

Sample Prayer:

Our Father, we gather to weep and mourn at your altar for those with the title of pastors and ministers who pervert your teaching. Our hearts break for those who have not submitted themselves to your molding and shaping. Some have dismissed the working of the Holy Spirit in their lives. While others have gone astray chasing meat for their bellies, eating the dainties of the world and deceiving your people by manipulating the scriptures for their own gain. In your wrath remember mercy. If you would count their iniquity, none could stand.

Despite their choices and decisions, grant them another opportunity to rend their hearts and seek a renewal of their minds. Receive those who cast their cares, burdens and fears at your feet. In your mercy, separate them from the familiar spirits, the mental challenges and the self-esteem insecurities that plagued them. May they run to your words of truth, hide in them and daily read them with the intent to digest the precepts found within. Help them admit they have fallen short of your glory. May repentance be a word that they embrace and not a word that they shun. Illuminate your truth over their lives and cause them to fall on the rock and avoid the rock falling on them.

Heavenly Father, guide them to a place where they see and recognize how they have perverted the gospel and have caused many to stumble. May they begin to weep and seek forgiveness from you and even the ones they have hurt. Bless them to be real before the congregation and cease from living a lie. May they willingly give up their positions, reconcile themselves to you by renewing their minds, and actively promote the complete healing of those they have hurt. May the members of the congregation be willing to forgive them even as you have forgiven them of their own trespasses. Through Christ we pray, amen.

> **Instructions For The Prayer Leader:**
>
> The leader will now call another person by name and instruct him or her to pray for pastors and ministers to preach the whole gospel.

Sample Prayer:

O' Lord our God, to you who sit upon the throne, be blessings, and honor, and wisdom, and power forevermore. We are your children, and we've gathered here to pray for a renewed mind in your pastors and ministers who preach the gospel. Thank you for giving us pastors after your own heart who teach your people wisdom and knowledge. As they abide in you, allow your words to abide in them, so that rivers of living water will flow out of their bellies.

Anoint these teachers of your word to teach without compromise or apology. Stir up truth within them. Allow the words of their mouth and the meditation of their heart to be acceptable in your sight. Quicken them to allow the words to be seasoned with salt and spoken with grace. Let it be like fire shut up in their bones. Like the prophet Jeremiah, let them not be able to remain silent when your Spirit burdens them with a now word. Speak through them great and mighty things they know not of as they open their mouths. Give them unction to speak the truth in love, without opinions or smooth enticing words. Direct them by your Holy Spirit to be God-pleasers rather than men-pleasers.

Father, bless your preachers to pursue knowing Christ and him crucified, not fads or the ideology of men. Let the word continue to transform their lives, that they may be bold, tenacious, and strong in the faith. Even when teased, mocked or ridiculed, let them be steadfast, unmovable and abound in the word. As the Apostle Paul testified, *"I am not ashamed of the gospel"*, let it be so with these preachers of righteousness. Let them believe in the gospel's power. So much so that they examine their own confession of faith.

May they never cease to pray for the people they minister to. Let their prayers be hot in their bosoms as they put on their whole armor to stand against the tricks of Satan. By your grace, allow these leaders to call to you in the morning, at noonday and at night. Guide them to pray all kinds of prayers to perfect your people for the work of the ministry. Bless them to obey the gospel so that they avoid your judgment. We believe and look with anticipation of you performing our request. For Christ's glory, amen.

> **Instructions For The Prayer Leader:**
>
> The leader will now call another person by name and instruct him or her to pray for our local pastors and ministers to demonstrate a transformed life as they preach the gospel.

Sample Prayer:

We appreciate the opportunity to lift up our pastors and ministers in our local church (insert name of your church) to you. May (insert your pastor and minister's names) continue to be led by your Holy Spirit to teach us the word in power and simplicity. Bless them to set aside quiet time to read, study, pray and prepare to teach us the truth. Be a shield for them against distractions that would seek to rob their intimacy with you. Bless our pastors and ministers to be transformed by the renewing of their minds to fulfill your divine assignment.

May our pastors and ministers approach teaching and preaching as a holy calling from you. Therefore, they approach the scripture as the inspired word of God, which is profitable unto men; the sacred desk as a holy place; and your people as your prized possessions. Lead them to present themselves as a living sacrifice, holy and acceptable to you. It is their reasonable service to be an example in their appearance as part of a royal priesthood, speaking words of life and truth, and living a life that worships and honors you. Help them be the servants you are molding them to be. Create in them a clean heart that dies to the flesh so that the old man remains dead.

Guide us to be discerning of their need for encouragement. May our congregation daily keep them and their families in prayer so that their feet will not slip from under them. By your Holy Spirit, give them a route of escape when the enemy would rush in like a flood. Set their feet upon the solid rock. Let them be like a tree planted by the rivers of water. Thank you for anchoring them in their identity in Christ. Establish them as leaders who are firmly planted in the scriptures and who continue to drink from the wellspring of life. Bless us to hear and apply the word they minister to us. In Jesus' name, amen.

Instructions For The Prayer Leader:

Prayer leader closes out prayer with thanksgiving (see Philippians 4:6) by faith that God will reward and give answers to meet the prayer request (see Hebrews 11:6).

Sample Closeout Prayer:

Father, we thank you that you hear us always. We have come in faith with full assurance that you cannot lie and that your words are true. You have already declared that if we ask anything according to your will, you will answer and grant us the petitions of our heart. Therefore, we give you thanks for transforming pastors and ministers who teach your word into vessels that rightly divide the word. We rejoice in the growth that will take place in your leaders and the impact that it will have on their families, community, co-workers and many others. Thank you for your faithfulness in performing your word. In Jesus' name, amen.

These prayers were based on the following scriptures:

1 Corinthians 2:1-5

1 Peter 4:16-17

Joel 2:13

Romans 3:23

Romans 12:1

Jeremiah 3:15

Colossians 4:6

Psalms 19:14

Galatians 2:20

Psalm 18:36

Isaiah 59:19

1 Timothy 3:16

Ephesians 6:11

Ephesians 4:11-12

MONTH 7

SUBMIT TO GOD

"Submit yourselves therefore to God. Resist the devil, and he will flee from you" (James 4:7)

The lack of godly submission among Christians is plaguing our nation. We have submitted ourselves to every evil thing to our own hurt. Ideologies of systemic racism, cancel culture, political correctness, have all led to a loss of our moral compass, a slide down every slippery slope, which has brought chaos, wickedness and destruction to the American family and faith in God. The prophet Jeremiah stated, *"the heart of men is desperately wicked"* (see Jeremiah 17:9). This wasn't just true in his day. This is definitely true today. Is there no balm in America? Yes, there is. When all men submit, surrender, and yield to God's authority over their lives, we will see a turning back to the narrow path that leads to life and it more abundantly. God has charged his church to lead the way in repentance and prayer. As the children of God submit and pursue a right relationship with God, the hand of mercy will cover the multitude of their sins. Judgment is coming, and it is coming first to the house of God. The Spirit of God is beseeching us to repent from allowing pride, selfishness, indifference and a lack of prayer to dominate our lives. Prayer must become our necessary food. Through submission and prayer, we cultivate a right relationship with God. God is waiting; sinful men are hanging in the balances and we that are called by his name must humble ourselves, pray, seek his face and turn from our wicked ways.

Week 1

Pray For Christians To Submit, Repent And Pray For A Right Relationship With God

Read: Isaiah 53:6a, Isaiah 1:13-18

Meditate on: Acts 3:19

Pray these verses: 2 Chronicles 7:14-15, 1 Thessalonians 5:17

Week 2

Pray For Those Blinded By The Culture To Be Enlightened With Truth And Submit To God

Read: Romans 8:5-8, 1 John 2:15-17

Meditate on: Romans 10:3

Pray these verses: Ephesians 1:18, James 4:7-10

Week 3

Pray For Sexually Misguided Individuals To Be Convicted of Sin And Submit To God

Read: Romans 1:21-32

Meditate on: Matthew 3:2

Pray these verses: Romans 6:19, James 4:6-10

Pray For Families To Awake, Submit To God And Pursue A Right Relationship With Him

Read: 2 Chronicles 33:1-2, 6, Proverbs 22:6

Meditate on: Joshua 24:15b

Pray these verses: Romans 13:11-14, James 4:7

Here is an example of corporate prayer for Month 7, Week 3

Pray For Sexually Misguided Individuals To Be Convicted of Sin And Submit To God

> **Instructions For The Prayer Leader:**
>
> The prayer leader should begin by reading the introduction followed by the subject for this time of prayer and the opening text (Romans 1:21-32). He or she may follow by defining what submission means. The emphasis in this month's corporate prayer is submitting to God for a right relationship. To submit is to yield or surrender yourself to the authority or will of God. On any given day, we unconsciously submit to many authority figures. We submit to workplace leaders, police officers, teachers if we are taking a class, doctors who

SUBMIT TO GOD

> **Instructions For The Prayer Leader continued:**
>
> prescribe medication for us and our parents, especially if we still live at home. Our relationship with the authority figure is often why we submit. Likewise, when we desire a better relationship with God, we will seek to be more mindful of his instructions and therefore are more willing to submit.
>
> The prayer leader may now read the scriptures to be prayed (Romans 6:19-25 and James 4:7-10) and invite everyone to gather in a circle, holding hands, to touch and agree as a demonstration of unity.
>
> The leader opens prayer with a brief covering prayer for this time of corporate prayer.

Sample Opening Prayer:

Father, we are so grateful to have this time to stand in the gap and pray for those who have not submitted to your will concerning their sexuality. We too have not always seen our bodies as the temple of God. Even as we stand in this circle, we ask for your mercy and forgiveness for our trespasses. We come to you as humbled vessels that recognize our own sinfulness. May we be focused on the purpose for which we have gathered to pray. Enable us to forget about ourselves and concentrate on the needs of others. Guide us with your Holy Spirit to have a heart of compassion and a burden for those who have strayed from submitting to your will for their lives. We take authority over any spirit that would try to hinder our submission to your will as we pray. We are your children who hear and obey your voice. We submit to your direction in what we should pray. Formulate the words that you want us to utter, so that the yoke would be destroyed in the lives of those Satan has bewitched. In Jesus' name, amen.

> **Instructions For The Prayer Leader:**
>
> The prayer leader will call on the first person who God has impressed upon him or her to pray that the flesh would not block those misguided in their sexuality from submitting to God (based on Romans 6:19-25).

Sample Prayer:

Father, we have gathered here to cry out to you for the individuals misguided in their sexuality. It pains us to know that the enemy has deceived them into believing they were created for some other purpose than what you intended. Despite the enemy enticing them to defile their bodies, Christ has come to liberate them. Help them, Lord, to resist yielding their eyes, hands and private parts to uncleanness. Deliver them from having sexual attraction and other inordinate affections towards those of the same sex. In spite of some having turned away from the natural design you created for them and having embraced doing their own thing, we ask you to renew a right spirit in them.

Father, we pray for those who profess to be Christians who struggle with same-sex attraction, pornography, cross-dressing, and other deviant sexual behavior. Help them to internalize your word, accept their new identity in Christ and to walk in the new man created in righteousness and holiness. Rise up in them mightily to cast down familiar spirits, resist situations that stir up the old man, and shun the appearance of evil. Jesus Christ, the greater one, lives in them and is able to give them the victory over all the wiles of the devil.

We believe the saving grace of Christ is able to silence the loud voice of their flesh. Let them no longer be motivated to satisfy the lust of their flesh. Bless them to choose the narrow path that leads to life and reject the wide road of destruction. Help them through your Holy Spirit to cast down vain imaginations that stir up the lust of their flesh and the pride of life. May they be quickened to reject the lies of the media, educational system, medicine and the politicians. Renew the Spirit of purity in these precious ones. Bless them to become servants of righteousness who submit their thoughts and bodies to you. May your will be done on earth in their life as it is in heaven. In Jesus' name, amen.

> **Instructions For The Prayer Leader:**
>
> The leader will now call another person by name and instruct him or her to pray for those who have rejected God's truth about their sexuality to resist the Devil (based on James 4:7-8) and draw near to God.

Sample Prayer:

Father, we take this moment to hallow your great name. You are worthy of all our praise and adoration. There is no other name under heaven whereby men can be saved other than Jesus. It is Jesus who has all the ability to deliver those who were bound by Satan, to make the captives free and to heal their brokenness.

We gather together to lift up those who have rejected God's truth about their sexuality. Father, you have promised to give grace unto all who humble themselves under your mighty hand. We stand in the gap and ask for your grace to be poured out upon those who have ignorantly rejected your words of truth. May their knees bow and their tongues confess that Jesus is Lord. Draw them to yourself and cause them to know the abundant life that is in Christ. Teach them the ways of your precept and cause them to know you are faithful and true and perfect in all of your ways. May they remember that God has not made a mistake when he formed them.

God has fearfully and wonderfully made them in his image and likeness. Father, you said they were good once you fashioned the man Adam and the woman Eve. Bless them to embrace the goodness you placed in them as a male or a female you created.

May your Spirit lead them to lay aside every sin and weight that so easily beset them. Allow whatever past hurts, misunderstanding, or lack of knowing God's love for them to cause them to draw near to you. Where they have defiled themselves, guide them to sound doctrine that will teach them how to cleanse their hands and purify their hearts. Open up their blind eyes, unstop their deaf ears and cause the truth to be pleasant unto them. Let them encounter truth everywhere they go. Send perfect laborers across their path to herald the Good News to them. Let them see a lie for what it is. Bring these boys, girls and adults to a place of submission. Cause them to trade their guilt and shame, resist the devil and draw near to God. Help them to realize their battle is not with flesh and blood, but with powers and principalities. As we pray, may they resist the Devil. In Jesus' name, amen.

> **Instructions For The Prayer Leader:**
>
> The leader will now call another person by name and instruct him or her to pray for humility in those who are sexually misguided (James 4:10) to override the spirit of pride.

Sample Prayer:

Our Father, we give you reverence and acknowledge that you are Lord over all. We ask you to forgive us for our prideful ways and to renew a humble spirit within us. We know you do not hear the prayers of sinners, so we take time to repent of any hidden pride in our own lives. Let nothing hinder us from coming to the throne of grace to ask help for those who have allowed pride to reign over them.

Father, in Jesus' name, we take authority over every prideful spirit that has sought a hiding place in the mind and heart of your people. May they recognize that pride has led them to the dark place they now find themselves. You did not create them to be perverse in their sexuality. Your plans for them, even now, are to give them hope and a future of blessings. Let the same spirit that was in Jesus be in them to cause them to humble themselves to honor you and follow in Christ's footsteps.

Deliver them from friendships and associations that corrupt and lead them astray. Stir them to embrace the wisdom of God and reject the leading of their peers. Shield from the peer pressure that is a constant bombardment through their eye and ear gates. Cause them to know that God resists the proud, but he gives grace to the humble. Thank you, Lord, for blessing those who were on a destructive path, to cast down every selfish attitude that exalts itself above you. In Jesus' name, amen.

Instructions For The Prayer Leader:

The prayer leader closes out the prayer with thanksgiving (see Philippians 4:6) by faith that God will reward and give answers to meet the prayer request (see Hebrews 11:6).

Sample Closeout Prayer:

Father, thank you for the opportunity to come to you to make our request known to you. You have promised not to withhold any good thing from those who walk uprightly before you. We confess that those who the Spirit is drawing through our prayers will no longer be confused about their sexual identity. They will return to a genuine submission to your purposes and plan for their life. We are confident that you hear us always and will grant our petitions. We know it is your will to deliver your people from the influence of Satan. Therefore, we know our petition will be answered. Thank you for breaking the shackles and chains off their minds. We rejoice, and again we rejoice, for your faithfulness in granting our petitions. Through Christ, amen.

These prayers were based on these scriptures:

Romans 6:19

John 8:32

John 10:10

1 Thessalonians 5:22

Psalm 139:14

1 John 2:16

Hebrews 12:1

Philippians 2:10

Isaiah 42:7

Ephesians 6:12

Jeremiah 29:11

James 4:6-10

MONTH 8

Trust God, He Is Faithful

"There hath no temptation taken you but such as is common to man: but God is faithful, who will not suffer you to be tempted above that ye are able; but will with the temptation also make a way to escape, that ye may be able to bear it" (1 Corinthians 10:13).

The Apostle Paul shares this profound word with the church at Corinth, God is faithful. By faithful, he meant God is consistently loyal, responsible, and devoted to his children by performing or fulfilling the promises that He has made to them. When we experience continued difficulties in our Christian walk, we sometimes allow our five senses to control our thinking. We walk by sight and feelings more than the Word of God. Adverse situations are unavoidable. An adversity is a continued state of hardship, affliction, misfortune, calamity or distress caused by Satan or by our own disobedience. Despite this temporary situation, God has already made provisions to deliver us out of our adversities way before we are even aware of them. God is faithful to deliver us if we trust him even when we can't track him. Though it may seem easy to conform to this world because of our adversity, trust in the Lord with all your heart; and lean not unto your own understanding. God is faithful to deliver.

Week 1

Pray For Christians to Trust God's Faithfulness When Fear Tries to Consume Them

Read: Job 1:14-19, Job 3:25-26

Meditate on: Psalm 9:9-10

Pray these verses: Psalm 34:15-22, 1 Peter 5:7

Week 2

Pray For Parents to Trust God's Faithfulness to Deliver Their Children When It Looks Impossible

Read: Mark 5:22-24, 35-43

Meditate on: Psalm 46:1-2

Pray these verses: Psalm 27:13-14, Psalm 55:22, Proverbs 3:5-6

Week 3

Pray For Christian Leaders to Trust God's Faithfulness for the Performance of the Vision for the Church

Read: Ezekiel 12:21-28

Meditate on: Psalm 84:11-12

Pray these verses: Psalm 37:3-7, Habakkuk 2:2-3

Week 4

Pray For Those With A Death Sentence From Men/Doctors/Society To Trust God's Faithfulness To Deliver

Read: Acts 28:1-6

Meditate on: Philippians 4:6-7

Pray these verses: Luke 10:19, 2 Corinthians 1:9-10

Here is an example of corporate prayer for Month 8, Week 4

Pray For Those With A Death Sentence From Men/Doctors/Society To Trust God's Faithfulness To Deliver

> **Instructions For The Prayer Leader:**
>
> The prayer leader should begin by reading the introduction followed by the subject for this time of prayer and the opening text (Acts 28:1-6). He or she may follow by defining what

TRUST GOD, HE IS FAITHFUL

> **Instructions For The Prayer Leader continued:**
>
> trust means. The emphasis in this month's corporate prayer is "Trust God; He Is Faithful". To trust God means to have full confidence in His promises because He cannot lie. Unlike men, God is consistently reliable, faithful and just. He doesn't change because we mess up. His faithfulness is great, and His plans for us are for good and not evil. His love for us assures us we are never alone, even in our darkest times.
>
> The prayer leader may now read the scriptures to be prayed (Luke 10:19, 2 Corinthians 1:9-10) and invite everyone to gather in a circle, holding hands, to touch and agree as a demonstration of unity.
>
> The prayer leader opens prayer with a brief covering prayer for this time of corporate prayer.

Sample Opening Prayer:

Father, we thank you for this time to draw near to you through prayer. Our hearts are full as we reflect on our own lack of trusting you. We take this time to ask for forgiveness and turn our hearts towards the needs of others as we pray. May the people who are on your heart who feel overwhelmed by their adversities sense our standing in the gap to pray for them. I ask you to cover each person here, surround us with your presence, fill us with your Spirit, and pray your will through us. We trust you to lead us and guide us as we pray for those who are fearful-hearted, facing a medical crisis, or facing a diagnosis of impending death. In Jesus's name, amen.

> **Instructions For The Prayer Leader:**
>
> The prayer leader will call on the first person who God has impressed upon him or her to pray for those who have received a negative health report from a doctor to trust God's faithfulness.

Sample Prayer:

Father, I thank you that eyes have not seen and ears have not heard what you are planning for those who love and trust you. We take this time to pray for those who have heard a negative report from man. Men speak death, but you speak life. May they believe your report over the report of men. Even if a thousand voices would speak words of death in their ears, let them hear your voice louder. You alone are the author and finisher of their faith. It is you who give life, and no man can take their gift of life from them apart from your doing. Open their eyes to see you working purpose in their diagnosis. May they not allow these reports of doom and gloom to distract them from your purposes for their lives.

We stand against all the works of darkness. Every fiery dart of the enemy will miss its target. You have promised to lift a standard when the enemy would rush in to plant seeds of doubt, fear, and discord. Expose Satan's lies for what they are. Shield the mind and heart of your people from the onslaught of thoughts contrary to your will. Enable them to cast down every imagination that would exalt itself against their knowledge of Christ. We confess no weapon formed against your beloved will prevail.

Shower them with your peace. Let their hearts not be troubled and frightened. Give them a sense of knowing they are in the palm of your hand. You have promised never to leave them or forsake them. Quicken them to trust you when their situation makes little sense. Enable them to confess you as their healer and deliverer. Shadrach, Meshach and Abednego trusted you to be with them in the fiery furnace. May those who love you trust you the same as the three Hebrew boys. May they exercise your power to tread down the enemy of their good health. Whatever the outcome, we have complete faith you will be with them to deliver them.

You are the Alpha and Omega, the first and the last; your word will stand even when the earth is removed or the flowers fade. Men do not have the last word. A diagnosis of cancer, cardiac failure, stroke, dementia and any other medical situation is subject to you, the living God. Even now, you can speak to these precious vessels and command them to come forth even as you did Lazarus. Many are the afflictions of the righteous, but you deliver them out of them all. Faithful are you that called them, and faithful are you to keep them. In Jesus' name, Amen.

> **Instructions For The Prayer Leader:**
>
> The leader will now call another person by name and instruct him or her to pray pray for those coming out of addictions to trust God and walk by faith.

Sample Prayer:

Lord Jesus, you are the resurrection and the life. The world has labeled those struggling with addictions as useless, a waste of time, and unredeemable. Jesus, you came for them that were lost and laden with sin and iniquity. Open the eyes of their understanding and let them be enlightened with the truth. As they seek to break free, send the right laborers to share the good news with them. We pray they will trust you and turn from the vices that once held them captive. Lord, take the smell out of their nostrils, the taste out of their mouths, and blind their eyes to the temptations that once help them captive. By your Holy Spirit, show them they are far more precious than sparrows. Keep them in your arms. Let them not be ashamed for trusting you.

Father, we pray for those who have received Christ as their Lord and Savior. You have given them power over all the works of the devil. May they put on their whole armor and stand against the plots of the enemy. When they are weak in the faith, strengthen them to confess your word and resist the devilish thoughts. Though their best friends have lied, abandoned and failed them, cause them to know you are not like men. You are faithful, kind and merciful. You are the God of another chance. Use their struggles to bring them to the place of dependence on you. Transform their minds through your written and preached word.

In your mercy, deliver those who have not received Jesus Christ into their hearts who are struggling with various addictions. Let them not charge you foolishly for their own failures or ignorance. Quicken them to grab hold of your love and surrender every aspect of their life to you. Surround them with people who love them and want the best for them. May they hear your still small voice and respond to your call to abandon the old life. We ask all these things in Jesus' name, amen.

> **Instructions For The Prayer Leader:**
>
> The leader will now call another person by name and instruct him or her to pray for family members to trust God for the healing of their loved ones.

Sample Prayer:

Father, there is nothing too hard for you through Jesus Christ. You healed many people and allowed it to be written to build our faith. Jairus's twelve-year-old daughter, who was dying, the woman with an issue of blood for twelve years, who spent all her money to no avail; the demon-possessed young child; and the Syrophenican woman's daughter, who was delivered from an unclean spirit. Jesus, there is no sickness or disease that is too difficult for you. You gave sight to blind Bartimaeus; you enabled the mute to speak, healed lepers, cured Simon's mother's fever, and cast out devils into swine. Lord, you healed them all according to your will, time and purpose.

Lord, hear our prayers. Throughout all the earth, you do not change. You are the Lord who heals us and our loved ones. May the families of these individuals who are sick have faith to believe in your track record. Stir them to come to you to do what is impossible with men. Bless them to cry day and night for their loved one's deliverance from the prognosis of men and the works of Satan. Show them great and mighty things they do not know.

May the spouses, mothers, fathers and relatives who trust you to heal their family member see your power and glory. Show them you are the rock that is higher than they.

Let them not be ashamed for putting their trust in you. When they face opposition, enable them to be strong in the power of your might. Be a shield for them and lift their heads. Block the fiery darts of discouragement, vain imaginations and evil speaking. We ask you to help them gird up the loins of their minds and think on things above. Enable them through your Spirit to accept how you choose to raise up their loved one. Cause them to know that all life is in your hand alone. Thank you for being the faithful God we can trust. In Jesus' name, amen!

> **Instructions For The Prayer Leader:**
>
> The prayer leader closes out the prayer with thanksgiving (see Philippians 4:6) by faith that God will reward and give answers to meet the prayer request (see Hebrews 11:6).

Sample Close Out Prayer:

Thanks be to God, who always causes us to triumph. We believe by faith that our prayer requests have been heard and are being answered. Where your people were fearful, troubled and perplexed, they are now peaceable, confident and steadfast in your promises. Father, we are thankful that we were able to bring our cares to the throne of grace. We rejoice in your manifested healing for your people. The works of the enemy have been routed, and the power of God has been released. We rejoice because God broke the chains, freed the captives, and restored health and healing to his people. We appreciate you always listening to us. In Jesus' name, amen.

These prayers were based on these scriptures:

Jeremiah 17:7, Jeremiah 33:3

Isaiah 40:7, Exodus 15:26

Jeremiah 17:14

Mark 8:26-56

Mark 15:25-37

Matthew 18:11

Ephesians 1:18

Numbers 23:19,

Psalm 3:3,

1 Peter 1:13

MONTH 9

SERVE GOD ACCEPTABLY

"Wherefore we receiving a kingdom which cannot be moved, let us have grace, whereby we may serve God acceptably with reverence and godly fear:" (Hebrews 12:28).

People credit Winston Churchill with the saying, *"Attitude is a little thing that makes a big difference"*. Our attitude (view, disposition, perspective, or outlook) of what it means to reverence God will determine what kind of service we render to God and to our fellow man. There are two basic ideas in the word "reverence": respect and fear. Our reverence for God should go beyond our respect and fear of any man. Since God alone is holy; then everyone and everything else must take a lesser seat or place of honor/respect/reverence. The scripture commands us, "serve God acceptably with reverence and godly fear". Let the attitude or mind that was in Christ be in you as well. It was Jesus' attitude of reverence for the Father that caused him to say, "nevertheless not my will, but thine, be done" (Luke 22:42). Only when we reach this place of not my will can we serve God acceptably with reverence and godly fear. Prayer is a key to cultivating an attitude of reverence and godly fear, which will lead us to serve God acceptably.

Week 1

Pray For Christians To Have An Attitude of Reverence In Hearing God's Word

Read: Nehemiah 8:1-11

Meditate On: Leviticus 20:26

Pray these verses: Psalm 89:7, Isaiah 55:3

Week 2

Pray For Sinners To Have An Attitude of Reverence And Godly Fear Towards God's Servants

Read: Matthew 21:33-39

Meditate On: Hebrews 12:9

Pray these verses: Romans 13:1-8

Week 3

Pray For Pastor's In (Your City) To Serve God Acceptably By Preaching The Whole Truth

Read: Acts 20:17-21

Meditate On: 1 Peter 3:15

Pray these verses: 1 Corinthians 9:16-23, 1 Corinthians 10:13

Week 4

Pray For Banking Industry To Serve God Acceptably In How They Deal With Their Customers

Read: Nehemiah 5:1-11

Meditate On: Romans 12:10

Pray these verses: Matthew 7:12, 1 Thessalonians 5:15

Here is an example of corporate prayer for Month 9, Week 2

Pray For Sinners To Have An Attitude of Reverence And Godly Fear Towards God's Servant

> **Instructions For The Prayer Leader:**
>
> The prayer leader should begin by reading the introduction followed by the subject for this time of prayer and the opening text (Matthew 21:33-39). He or she may follow by defining what reverence means.

SERVE GOD ACCEPTABLY

> **Instructions For The Prayer Leader continued:**
>
> The emphasis in this month's corporate prayer is, "Serve God Acceptably". To have reverence toward someone conveys a feeling of deep regard, honor and respect; especially toward God. Acceptably means meeting a need, requirement, or standard that is worthy of being received by the recipient. So, we are to honor God by presenting him with things he requires or desires.
>
> The prayer leader may now read the scriptures to be prayed (Romans 13:1-8) and invite everyone to gather in a circle, holding hands, to touch and agree as a demonstration of their unity.
>
> The prayer leader opens prayer with a brief covering prayer for this time of corporate prayer.

Sample Opening Prayer:

Father, we appreciate the opportunity to gather to stand in the gap for others. We ask for forgiveness of our sins. May each person here fix his or her attention on the mission that lies ahead of us. We put on our whole armor and draw our swords ready to wage a good warfare. Holy Spirit, you are welcome and invited to lead us and guide us to pray Father's will. Give us the compassion, the love and the words to pray. Direct our prayers, knit our hearts together in unity and enable us to be a powerful force against the enemy. Thank you in advance for delivering the unsaved from the powers of darkness. In Jesus' name, amen.

> **Instructions For The Prayer Leader:**
>
> The prayer leader will call on the first person who God has impressed upon him or her to pray for sinners to be open and receptive to the gospel message.

Sample Prayer:

Almighty God, you do not desire that anyone should perish. It is your desire that all men and women would come to the saving knowledge of Jesus Christ. We bring before you family members, friends, co-workers, neighbors, and those we do not know you personally as well as those deceived by Satan and drowning in their sins. May the eyes of their understanding be enlightened with the truth, and may their hearts be receptive of your love. Quicken them to know your plans for their lives and the depths of your love. Father, you have an expected end for their lives. They are not mistakes or useless. Bless them to hear with their ears and see with their eyes the truth of the gospel.

Let every soul be subject unto your Holy Spirit. Forgive these precious ones who are living contrary to your plans for their lives. Though they believe what they are doing and how they are living is right, it is still wrong in your sight. Some have trusted in their own might and have ignored your precepts. Open their eyes, unstop their ears and cause them to know your ways are best. Let their pursuits lead them to a Damascus Road experience that causes them to know you are Lord. Cause their knees to bow and their tongues to confess that Jesus is Lord. Grant them a change of attitude and behavior. Let them not be able to turn to the right or the left as you are drawing them. In the midnight hour, during the day and at night, may your words of life be ever before them. Nothing and no one is too hard for you to deliver out of the clutches of the Devil. By faith, we believe that each person you are drawing will submit to your will and receive your gift of eternal life. Father, save them, and they will be saved. Through and because of Christ we pray, amen.

> **Instructions For The Prayer Leader:**
>
> The leader will now call another person by name and instruct him or her to pray for sinners to have respect for those who are God's representatives who minister to them.

Sample Prayer:

Yours, O' Lord, is the power and the glory. There is no one like you. May those who are not of the fold have respect for your representatives. Quicken them to give honor to those who hazard their lives to preach, teach and share the gospel with them. Enable your ministers to live in such a way that sinners will see their good works and glorify you. Let none of your servants hide their light under a bushel from those who are seeking to find you. May the evangelists, ministers and pastors hide in Christ so the ungodly will see you and not them. Allow your spoken word through your servants to be as an arrow that hits the bullseye in the lives of those who are resisting your power.

Father, it is good that you have strategically placed your servants in the midst of those whom you are inviting to be a part of your family. Those who are hurting, abandoned and feeling hopeless, may they know through your servants' actions that you love them. Allow your ministers to be your hands that reach out to the broken, and your shoulders to give them somewhere to lean their heads. Reveal the depth of your care for those struggling to hear and obey the instructions of your servants. May the doubt, fear and lies of Satan fall away as you loving use your ministers to meet their needs. As your servants serve you acceptably with reverence, may the sinner imitate them and serve you with reverence. We ask all these things in Jesus' name, amen.

SERVE GOD ACCEPTABLY

> **Instructions For The Prayer Leader:**
>
> The leader will now call another person by name and instruct him or her to pray for sinners to have an attitude of repentance and serve God acceptably.

Sample Prayer:

Lord Jesus, your word reminds us that all have sinned and come short of your glory. There is no man or woman who has not sinned. We pray for conviction to come upon the sinner. Stir them in the inward parts to have godly sorrow. Even as King David recognized it was only against you, he had sinned, may the sinner also recognize that their actions, attitude and behavior disappoint you and separate them from you. May they seek to be restored to a right relationship with you.

Father, your mercy is from everlasting to everlasting to those who fear you. In your wrath remember mercy. Do not give the sinner what they deserve, but allow them another opportunity to repent. If you would count their iniquities, they would not be able to stand. So, burden their heart to turn from sin and to turn to you. Renew a right spirit and create a clean heart in them. May they be sincere and without offense as they ask for forgiveness. See their hearts and remove anything that would come in the way of their running to the mercy seat. Put their sin as far as east is to west and blot out their transgressions.

Father, your word declares that if we confess our sins, you are faithful and just to forgive us. Your word cannot lie, and all your promises are yea, and in you, amen. May the sinner trust your track record and believe your word. Enable them by your Spirit to humble themselves, and pray, and seek your face, and turn from their wicked ways. For there is no one else who can cleanse them from all unrighteousness but you. As you lead them beside still waters, may they choose to serve you with their whole heart and soul. Reveal to them that they were created for your good pleasure. Though they may have strayed from your plans, your purposes and plans still stand and will come to pass. We thank you for hearing our prayers and attending to their pleas. In the name of Jesus, amen.

> **Instructions For The Prayer Leader:**
>
> The prayer leader closes out the prayer with thanksgiving (see Philippians 4:6) by faith that God will reward and give answers to meet the prayer request (see Hebrews 11:6).

Sample Close Out Prayer:

Father, we thank you for hearing our prayers. We have confidence that you have answered our petitions. You are a rewarder of those who diligently seek you. So, by faith we have sought you on behalf of those who were bound in sin. We are grateful that you provided a Savior and are supplying the needs of those the enemy has deceived. Thank you for doing what eyes have not seen nor ears heard. We are excited about your purposes for those you are drawing to yourself. The shackles have been broken from their minds, hearts, feet and hands. Thank you for bringing them into your family. We rejoice in the transformation they will experience. They will never be the same, nor will they return to the old life. Whom the Son makes free will be free indeed. We call them free from sin. In Jesus' name, amen.

These prayers were based on these scriptures:

Ephesians 1:18

2 Peter 3:9

Romans 14:11

Jeremiah 32:17

Matthew 5:16

Romans 3:23

2 Corinthians 7:10

Jeremiah 29:11

Psalm 51:1-4

Psalm 103:8-12

1 John 1:9

2 Chronicles 7:14

Ephesians 2:10

Psalm 23:2

Month 10

BE HOLY; FOR I AM HOLY

*"But as he which hath called you is holy, so be ye **holy in all manner** of conversation; Because it is written, **Be ye holy; for I am holy**"* (1 Peter 1:15-16).

The Body of Christ has moved away from acknowledging God's holiness. Some are blind to God's holiness; others are ignorant; and still there is a group of professors who say holiness was for the Old Testament saints. As a result, there is no daily life of reverence, respect, or honor for God, his people or his church. This lack of understanding directly impacts our Christian faith, our walk and, most of all, our relationship with God. Without holiness, all our actions, behavior and living will be fruitless, empty words and lifeless works. Holy is who God is. He is the creator, the source of life, sinless, morally pure and distinct from everything else. Religion, church attendance, giving offerings, religious jargon or clothing can't make you holy. No person can determine who or what is holy except for God. He has made you holy when you received his Son by putting his Holy Spirit in you. Therefore, you have everything you need to be holy. Now he asks you to perfect the holiness he gave you. Holiness is not an option. It is a requirement for a child of God. Godly men like Isaiah, Job, Elijah and John responded to God's presence with a sense of awe and repentance. Despite our sin, God has by his grace made himself available to us; for this we should be in reverential fear, abstain from all evil and present ourselves holy and acceptable to him. It is our reasonable service to strive to be holy as He is holy.

Week 1

Pray For Christians To Hear Sound Doctrine And Live A Holy Life Based On The Scriptures

Read: 1 Thessalonians 2:8-13

Meditate On: Luke 11:28

Pray these verses: 2 Timothy 3:16, James 1:19-22

Week 2

Pray For Worship Leaders To Humble Themselves And Praise God In The Beauty of His Holiness

Read: John 4:21-24, Revelations 4:8-11

Meditate On: Romans 12:1

Pray these verses: Psalm 29:2, Psalm 95:1-7a, 1 Peter 2:9

Week 3

Pray For Church Leaders To Forget Religious Church Traditions And Pursue Holiness

Read: Mark 7:6-13

Meditate on: 2 Timothy 1:9

Pray these verses: Exodus 19:6, Ephesians 4:22-24, 2 Timothy 4:2-5

Week:4

Pray For Sinners To Be Arrested By God's Holiness, Seek Repentance And Pursue Holiness

Read: Luke 19:1-10

Meditate On: Ephesians 1:4

Pray these verses: Psalm 51:1-4, 1 Peter 1:13-16

Here is an example of corporate prayer for Month 10, Week 1

Pray For Christians To Hear Sound Doctrine And Live A Holy Life Based On The Scriptures

BE HOLY; FOR I AM HOLY

> **Instructions For The Prayer Leader:**
>
> The prayer leader should begin by reading the introduction followed by the subject for this time of prayer and the opening text (1 Thessalonians 2:8-13). He or she may follow by defining what holy means.
>
> Holy is who God is. So, to be holy means to take on the attributes of God and to live in his image and likeness according to the guidance of Holy Spirit. The emphasis in this month's corporate prayer is, "Be Holy".
>
> The prayer leader will now read the scriptures to be prayed (2 Timothy 3:16 and James 1:19-22) and invite everyone to gather in a circle, holding hands, to touch and agree to show their unity.
>
> The leader opens prayer with a brief covering prayer for this time of corporate prayer.

Sample Opening Prayer:

Our God and our Father, we thank you for the ability to approach the throne of grace in our time of need. We acknowledge we are needy and you alone are holy. We willingly give you the reverence, respect and honor that is due unto your holy name. Please forgive us for any sins that we have committed against you that would prevent you from hearing us. Look upon us and hear our supplications for Christians to hear sound doctrine and live according to the Holy Scriptures. May each person gathered here concentrate on the leading and guiding of the Holy Spirit to pray. Quicken each of us to put off the old man, and give us a heart of compassion for those in Christ who have forsaken living holy lives before you. We now take time to put on our whole armour that we may stand against the powers of darkness and fight the good fight in prayer. We gather in faith and with confidence that you will answer our petitions. In Jesus' name, amen.

> **Instructions For The Prayer Leader:**
>
> The prayer leader will call on the first person who God has impressed upon him or her to pray for Christians to repent for not living a holy life.

Sample Prayer:

Father, we come before you, knowing that we are guilty of not living a holy life. You have commanded every believer to be holy as you are holy, and yet we have not sought to obey the scriptures. We confess whatever has blocked our ears, darkened our understanding, blinded our eyes, and hardened our hearts will no longer have dominion over us.

We stand in the gap and pray that others as well as us would hear and obey your small, still voice.

O' Lord, forgive Christians for allowing the adversary to deceive them into thinking that holiness is not for them today. We all have sinned and fallen short of your holiness. A filthy heart and dirty hands cannot stand before you, the holy God. Christians have forgotten who you are. You are pure, blameless, and sinless. Your eyes are too pure to behold evil. Have mercy upon them and forgive their sin, for it is only against you they have sinned. Nothing is hidden from you. You see everything we do, say, and think. By your Spirit, equip your chosen to "touch not" or "handle not" the things that would prevent them from being holy vessels unto you. Blot out their sins, cast them into the sea and remember them no more. Hide your people in your holiness and enable them with the help of the Holy Spirit to strip off all the weight and sin that was besetting them.

Holy Spirit, we invite you to remind Christians to lay aside every wicked way and thought so that they can depend on Christ and not be independent of him. Forgive them when they forget they are God's children, created in righteousness and true holiness. Lead them beside still waters and into green pastures. We believe you will answer our prayers in Jesus' name, amen.

> **Instructions For The Prayer Leader:**
>
> The leader will now call another person by name and instruct him or her to pray for Christians to live a holy life by listening to and obeying the scriptures.

Sample Prayer:

O' give thanks unto the Lord, for his merciful kindness endures forever, and his truth to all generations. We are thankful you have not allowed your wrath to be upon us. Thank you, that your compassions fail not. Father, you have given us ears to hear, preachers to preach, and your Holy Spirit to convict and teach us your word. Help us hear what the Spirit is saying so that we can be doers of the word. Your commandments are not grievous. You have given us what we need to be holy as he is holy.

Holiness is what you want from us. Transform us through the renewing of our minds by the word of God. Even as the priest Ezra read the scrolls and the people stood attentive and patient to hear the recorded words, may we, your people, delight to hear what you require and then become doers of your word. Quicken us to be swift to hear and slow to speak.

Father, thank you for Jesus showing us how we are to live and honor your holiness. It was Jesus's meat to do your will. Help us lay down our preferences, take up our cross and follow in his footsteps. Not as we will, but let your Spirit work through us to do your will. We do not want to have a form of godliness. Let the scriptures we hear cause us to do what is right in your sight.

Restore within us a hunger and thirst for your righteous and holy ways. By your Spirit, cause us to receive the engrafted word of truth, which can save our souls. We confess we will be holy as you are holy and do your word. Thank you for another opportunity to listen and obey you. In Jesus' name, amen.

> **Instructions For The Prayer Leader:**
>
> The prayer leader closes out the prayer with thanksgiving (see Philippians 4:6) by faith that God will reward and give answers to meet the prayer request (see Hebrews 11:6).

Sample Close Out Prayer:

We thank you, Father, for answering our prayers and healing the sick. By faith, we believe Christians are returning to their first love and honoring you with a holy life. Even as the angels cried out, *"holy, holy, holy, Lord God Almighty"*, we believe they are seeing you as holy. Your words taste as sweet as honey and brings joy to your people. We rejoice that your mercy endures forever and you are the God of another chance. Thank you for your open arms that invites us to run to you. By faith, we trust you to perform your promises. In Jesus' name, amen.

These prayers were based on these scriptures:

Habakkuk 1:13

1 Samuel 15:23

Psalm 23:2

Isiah 55:3

Lamentations 3:22-23

Proverbs 14:34

Romans 12:1

James 1:19-22

Ephesians 4:24

Hebrews 12:1

Psalm 51

Revelations 4:8

MONTH 11

Live A Biblical Worldview

"Thy word is a lamp unto my feet, and a light unto my path" (Psalm 119:105).

The authority of Scripture means every word and stroke of the Bible possesses the authority of God and the right to rule the hearts, minds, and bodies of every inhabitant of the earth. Scripture's authority doesn't depend on whether people cooperate with it or understand it. Its authority depends on the power and supremacy of its Author—God. Because the Bible is the very Word of God, it is the ultimate authority in all matters of faith and life. Therefore, a bona fide Christian accepts the written word as inspired by God and lives by it. Living a biblical worldview reflects our relationship with Jesus Christ and requires ongoing self-examination, prayer, and obedience to the scriptures. The worldview is contrary to all that is holy, godly and moral. The Holy Spirit has equipped Christians to live a biblical worldview according to God's Word and not according to the will or ideology of men. As we allow God's word to be a lamp unto our feet and a light unto our path, the scriptures will always enable us to live with a biblical worldview.

Week 1

Live A Biblical Worldview By Allowing The Word Of God To Be The Final Authority

Read: 2 Timothy 3:14-17

Mediate on: Psalm 119:105

Pray these verses: 2 Corinthians 1:20, Joshua 1:8

Week 2

Live A Biblical Worldview By Loving God More More Than Loving The World

Read: Matthew 22:37-40, 2 Timothy 3:1-5

Meditate on: 1 John 5:2

Pray these verses: 1 John 2:15-17

Week: 3

Live A Biblical Worldview By Keeping Yourself Unspotted From The World

Read: Proverbs 1:10-16, 1 Corinthians 15:33

Meditate on: 2 Timothy 2:16

Pray these verses: Romans 12:1-2, 2 Corinthians 6:14-18, James 1:27

Week 4

Live A Biblical Worldview By Resisting Sin

Read: Genesis 39:2-12

Mediate on: 1 Corinthians 15:34

Pray these verses: Romans 13:11-14, 1 John 3:4-9

Here is an example of corporate prayer for Month 11, Week 2

Pray For Christians To Live A Biblical Worldview By Loving God More Than Loving The World

> **Instructions For The Prayer Leader:**
>
> The prayer leader should begin by reading the introduction followed by the subject for this time of prayer and the opening text (Matthew 22:37-40 and 2 Timothy 3:1-5). He or she may follow by defining a Biblical worldview.
>
> A Biblical worldview is based on viewing everything and addressing all things through

LIVE A BIBLICAL WORLDVIEW

> **Instructions For The Prayer Leader continued:**
>
> God's word, principles and guidance of the Holy Spirit.
>
> The emphasis in this month's corporate prayer is, "Live A Biblical Worldview". The prayer leader will now read the scriptures to be prayed (1 John 2:15-17) and invite everyone to gather in a circle, holding hands, to touch and agree to show their unity.
>
> The leader opens prayer with a brief covering prayer for this time of corporate prayer.

Sample Opening Prayer:

Our Father, who art in heaven, holy is your name. We are thankful to be summoned in this place to offer prayers and supplications on behalf of all people to love you more than the things of the world. We ask for forgiveness of our sin; for we know you do not hear the prayers of those practicing sin. May each person that is here be focused on our assignment and attentive to the leading and guiding of your Holy Spirit. We come to you believing that you are a rewarded of those who diligently seek you. By faith we set our heart and thoughts to wage a good warfare against the efforts of Satan to deceive your people to love the things he has to offer more than loving you. May we be used to stand in the gap and pray with fervency and confidence for the heart of your people to be tender and their mind to be renewed. In Jesus' name, amen.

> **Instructions For The Prayer Leader:**
>
> The prayer leader will call on the first person who God has impressed upon him or her to pray for prodigal sons and daughters along with those who love the world to repent and turn to God.

Sample Prayer

Father, the God of this world has enticed, blinded and trapped some who profess to be Christians and those who never invited you into their lives to love things more than you. The lust of the flesh, the lust of the eyes and the pride of life has robbed them from experiencing your peace and love. Their worldview has led them to be consumed by self-interest, self-sufficiency, and greed. Forgive them, for they know not what they do. In their efforts to live like the Joneses, they have compromised their values and abandoned their knowledge of you. Some people have ended up in the pigpen, others have lost their possessions, and some are weary of well-doing. Nothing material is ever enough for them. May their up-and-down living become exhausting for them. To live is Christ, and to die to the flesh is gain.

May they recognize that Christ alone is the answer. Open the eyes of their heart, turn them from darkness to light, and deliver them from the power of Satan. Help them know the love of God, which passes all understanding. Father, pour out your grace upon them to save them. Instruct them and teach them your ways. Lord, guide them with your watchful eye and lead them with your grace and mercy. Be a present help for them and bring them out of the miry clay and set their feet upon the rock. When nothing else seems to work in their life, let your love lift them. In Jesus' name, amen.

> **Instructions For The Prayer Leader:**
>
> The leader will now call another person by name and instruct him or her to pray for Christians to love God and remain strong against the temptation of the world.

Father, we love you; we worship and adore you. We pray for Christians to be quickened in the inward man to remember no one has loved them and sacrificed for them the way you have. You gave your only begotten Son to pay the price they could not. May born-again believers return the unconditional love you have shown them. Cause their love for you to be on display daily. You have commanded your children to love the Lord their God with all their heart, soul, and mind. May they choose to love you, because your commandments are not grievous. For Christians who love God, every trial will work together for their good and for your purposes.

Holy Spirit, help Christians to deny themselves, take up their cross, and follow Jesus. The life they now live, they live by faith in the Son of God. May they be like Joseph and run from sin and all the temptations of the world. No matter how enticing, they will be strong in the Lord and in the power of his might. Bless them to cast down all imaginations and every high thing that exalts itself against their knowledge of God and set their affections on things above. All they have come from you, Lord. The apostle Paul declared he was not ashamed of the gospel. May Christians also testify in word and deed that they love you. Thank you for holding Christians in the palm of your hand and being a shield for them against the plots of Satan. In Jesus' name, amen.

> **Instructions For The Prayer Leader:**
>
> The prayer leader closes out the prayer with thanksgiving (see Philippians 4:6) by faith that God will reward and give answers to meet the prayer request (see Hebrews 11:6).

Sample Close Out Prayer:

Father, we thank you for hearing our request and answering our petitions. We are so glad for this opportunity to stand in the gap for others in prayer. The opportunity to fulfill your command to always pray has blessed our life. We have no doubt you listened, and we believe you approved of our selfless prayers. With anticipation and expectation, we look forward to hearing testimonies of your intervention in the lives of your children. Thank you for releasing them from captivity and leading them back to you, their first love. We appreciate being included in your kingdom and receiving a kingdom assignment. In Jesus' name, amen.

These prayers were based on these scriptures:

Ephesians 2:8

Psalm 32:8

Acts 26:18

Psalm 40:2

Philippians 1:21

Mark 8:34

John 3:16

Genesis 39:12

Romans 1:16

2 Corinthians 10:5

MONTH 12

LET US TAKE THIS CITY

And from the days of John the Baptist until now the kingdom of heaven suffereth violence, and the violent take it by force" (Matthew 11:12).

Prayer undergirds every great move of God. Christians desperately need a revival. The decline of prayer, a deficient education system, the absence of the Ten Commandments in government, and judicial overreach have fueled the lawlessness gripping our streets. The ungodly seem to increase, and their evil works intrude in every area of our cities. As part of the church of the Lord Jesus Christ, the prayer warriors stand as watchmen upon the walls of our cities to call on Jesus' day and night. We are to give God's ears no rest until people are reconciled to God, the fear of God fills hearts, evildoers are illuminated by the truth and Satan's works are exposed, routed and stopped. Let us take this city (name of your city) by intercessory prayer and evangelism. It is our duty as repairers of the breach to take authority over all the works of the enemy. We are part of the special forces in the army of God, using intercessory prayer as our greatest weapon against all the forces of evil. Prayer is the battle plan to invite the Prince of Peace into our cities.

Week 1

Pray For Christians To Oppose Religious Spirits Operating In Their Cities

Read: Acts 17:16-32, Titus 1:10-16

Meditate on: James 4:7

Pray these verses: Luke 10:19, Titus 2:11-15

Week 2

Resist The Influence of Ungodly Legal And Illegal Businesses (Gambling, Drug, Strip Club, Money Laundering) **In Your City**

Read: Acts 16:16-20

Meditate on: 1 Timothy 5:20

Pray these verses: 2 Corinthians 10:3-5, 1 Thessalonians 5:14-15

Week 3

Speak Life Into The Dry Bones Resulting From Using Drug/Alcohol/Pornography/Tik-Tok In Your City

Read: Ezekiel 37:1-14

Meditate on: Proverbs 18:21

Pray these verses: Zechariah 8:16-17, Acts 4:29-31

Week 4

Liberate And Reclaim The Captives In Your Neighborhood For Christ

Read: Romans 3:9-18

Meditate on: Ephesians 1:18

Pray these verses: Isaiah 1:18-20, Isaiah 55:6-7

Here is an example of corporate prayer for Month 12, Week 4

Pray To Liberate And Reclaim The Captives In Your Neighborhood For Christ

---

Instructions For The Prayer Leader:

The prayer leader should begin by reading the introduction followed by the subject for this time of prayer and the opening text (Romans 3:9-18).

The emphasis in this month's corporate prayer is, "Let Us Take This City".

LET US TAKE THIS CITY

> **Instructions For The Prayer Leader continued:**
>
> The prayer leader may now read the scriptures to be prayed (Isaiah 1:18-20, and Isaiah 55:6-7) and invite everyone to gather in a circle, holding hands, to touch and agree as a demonstration of unity.
>
> The leader opens prayer with a brief covering prayer for this time of corporate prayer.

Sample Opening Prayer:

Our God, who is faithful and just, we gather to pray for our city. Lord, you know how our city has fallen into idolatry and forsaken your commandments. Our local leaders have embraced the culture and resist godliness, sound reason and doing what is right for its citizens. We ask you for souls to be saved as we fix our hearts to pray for those who have not asked for your mercy and forgiveness. May all gathered here feel compassion for those lost in sin. May tears run down our eyes when we consider their state. It is not your desire for them to perish, but to receive life and it more abundant. Use us by your Spirit to pray for the strongholds in their lives to be broken and the captives to be made free. Our heart's desire is for them to cry out, *"Lord save me"*. Thank you for this opportunity to approach your throne of grace. In Jesus' name, amen.

> **Instructions For The Prayer Leader:**
>
> The prayer leader will call on the first person who God has impressed upon him or her to pray for sinners in our neighborhood to be burdened by their sin and turn to Christ.

Sample Prayer:

Father, you have given us power over all the works of the enemy. We do not underestimate our foe lightly. Therefore, we put on our whole armour to stand against his influence over those he has taken captive in our city. We stand in unity with our swords drawn and declare, we will not back down from our assignment to pray until something happens. Our fight is not against flesh and blood, but against powers and principalities. Jesus has already made an open show of Satan and has taken the keys of hell and death.

Holy Spirit, we ask you to visit the men and women in our neighborhood who have submitted themselves to the lies of Satan. Some believe they are doomed and unable to break free; others blame themselves for their poor decisions; and still there are those who have given up resisting the sin that draws them. These precious ones are not invisible, as some may think.

You see them, though others may walk past them, turn their eyes away or ignore them as if they don't exist.

We command the enemy to loose the shackles from the minds of the ignorant and the deceived. Though their sins be like scarlet, God will make them white as snow. Holy Spirit, cause them to be willing and obedient to the voice of the Lord. Open their ears and hearts to the laborers who share the good news with them. Let their sin be heavy on their hearts and cause them to desire to be free. Let not rebellion and a hard head turn them away from the only hope available to them. Impress upon them to lift their eyes unto you, who are available and waiting to offer them help in their time of need. Guide them to cast their cares upon you because you care for them. Though they have fallen many times, enable them to rely upon you and sell all to follow you. This time will not be like other times. The whole host of heaven encamps around those who are heirs of salvation. We thank you that the blind will see, the deaf will hear and the dumb will speak of you. In Jesus' name, amen.

> **Instructions For The Prayer Leader:**
>
> The leader will now call another person by name and instruct him or her to pray for those bound by sin to seek God.

Father, you began a good work in these precious ones when you gave them breath and life. It is your desire to perform your good work in their lives. Your plan for them is to prosper and give them hope and a future of blessings as part of your family. Draw the sinner into your presence. Let no one be able to resist your lovingkindness. Visit them in the alleys, on the streets, in their homes, in their corporate offices, and even in their hiding places. Cause your voice to be louder than all the other voices they hear.

May the wicked forsake their ways and seek God while he is near. We believe as they abandon their ways and their ungodly thoughts, God will abundantly pardon them. Open their ears to hear you calling them to yourself. Quicken them to abstain from every appearance of evil. Help them press toward the mark of the high calling which is in Christ Jesus.

We confess the promises of God over the lives of those who are in dire situations. The weapons formed against them to destroy them will not prosper. The number of their days is in God's hands. Satan may have rented them for a season, but he cannot have them. God owns them; Jesus' shed blood purchased them, and they are redeemed from the law's curse. No sin is too great for our God to forgive. Whenever they seek your mercy, Father, we thank you that you will pour it out on them. We declare them to be free to walk in God's ways, to repent and cast off the works of old. We see new men and women in Christ accepting their place in God's family. God's power will help them fulfill his purposes and plans for their lives. In Jesus' name, amen.

> **Instructions For The Prayer Leader:**
>
> The prayer leader closes out the prayer with thanksgiving (see Philippians 4:6) by faith that God will reward and give answers to meet the prayer request (see Hebrews 11:6).

Sample Close Out Prayer:

Thanks be to God, who always causes us to triumph in him. We thank you for saving countless souls from Satan's grasp. We rejoice and are glad that you are the miracle-working God. No longer shall the streets be unsafe and people be fearful-hearted to interact with each other. The presence of the Lord is over our communities. The atmosphere is no longer filled with the oppression of darkness. We are thankful that we invited the King of Glory into our city; he came and blessed those who prayed and those who were prayed for. In Jesus' name, amen.

These prayers were based on these scriptures:

Ephesians 6:11

Isaiah 1:18-20

Jeremiah 29:11

1 Thessalonians 5:22

Isaiah 55:6-7

1 Peter 5:7

Hebrews 1:14

Philippians 3:14

Galatians 3:13

Psalm 121:1

1 Peter 1:5

FINAL THOUGHTS

My prayer is that every church and small group that desires to be a sharpshooter in the ministry of prayer would use this tool as an instructional guide to respond to the Holy Spirit and pray more effectively.

I believe the Holy Spirit has shown us the urgent need to recommit to corporate prayer and to claim God's Word and promises through our prayers. A deliberate return to corporate prayer is essential to uplift Christ, the church, and God's people to their rightful place in society, as repairers of the breach. The early church had regular times for corporate intercessory church prayer. The apostles practiced smaller group corporate prayer. Both examples are to be duplicated by twenty-first-century believers.

This guide summarizes the lessons Jesus taught his disciples concerning prayer. *"For where two or three are gathered together in my name, there am I in the midst of them"* (Matthew 18:20). God is not looking for a crowd. He is looking for a few committed men and women to stand in the gap and pray his word. He has already promised to be in our gathering and to answer any prayer request that is in his will. This workbook provides the resources, tools, examples, and scriptures you need to establish corporate prayer in the church or in a small group.

ABOUT THE AUTHOR

The author of this prayer manual is the Holy Spirit of God. He has inspired and directed the words penned on each page. His works speak for themselves throughout the entire Bible and the lives of the saints of God. He makes intercession for us with groanings which cannot be uttered. Further enabling every person to know what to pray, when to pray and how to pray.

About The Co-Author

Dr. Melrose Blake-Bethea dedicates and commits herself to living a life of prayer and intercession. She developed the intercessory prayer ministry at God's Life Christian Church and has overseen this ministry for over twenty-five years. Over the years she authors a monthly prayer focus for GLCC. She also has ministered, taught and trained many groups on developing an effective corporate prayer ministry.

Dr. Bethea's husband is Bishop Calvin Bethea, who is the founder and senior pastor at God's Life Christian Church in Irvington, NJ and Ewa Beach, Hawaii. She assists him in teaching and training believers for the work of the ministry. She is dedicated and committed to living a life of prayer and intercession.

In her effort to feed and pray for the body of Christ, Dr. Bethea is co-owner of Hawaii Christian Outlet (HCO). HCO is a Christian Bookstore and Christian resource center with a mission to equip believers of all ages. She is author of "Divine Interruptions" a book that enable believers to prepare and address interruptions in their life.

www.ingramcontent.com/pod-product-compliance
Lightning Source LLC
Chambersburg PA
CBHW081500070526
44586CB00019B/2437